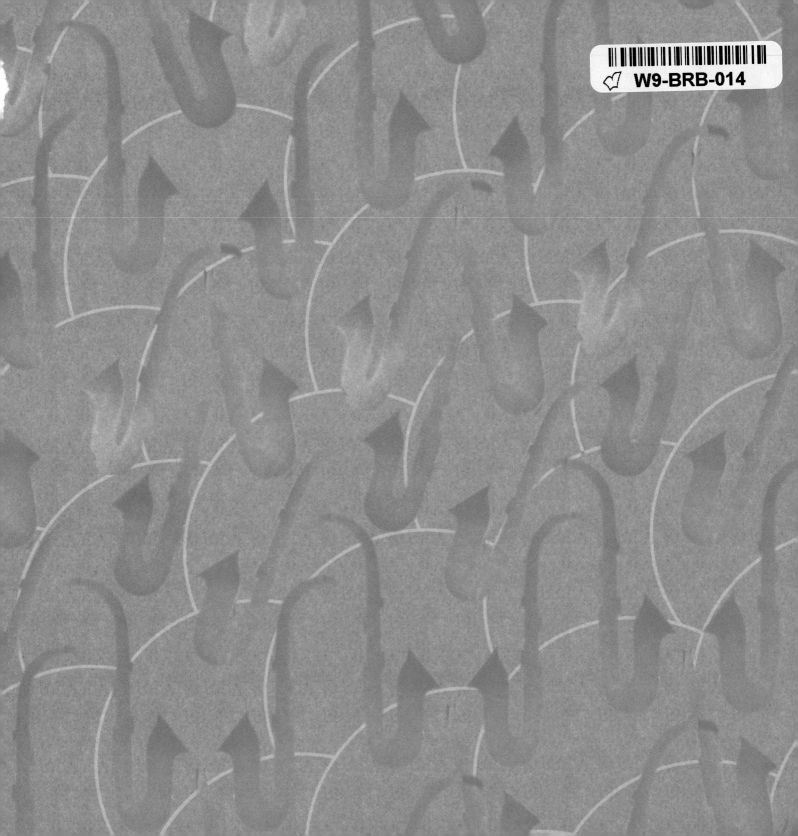

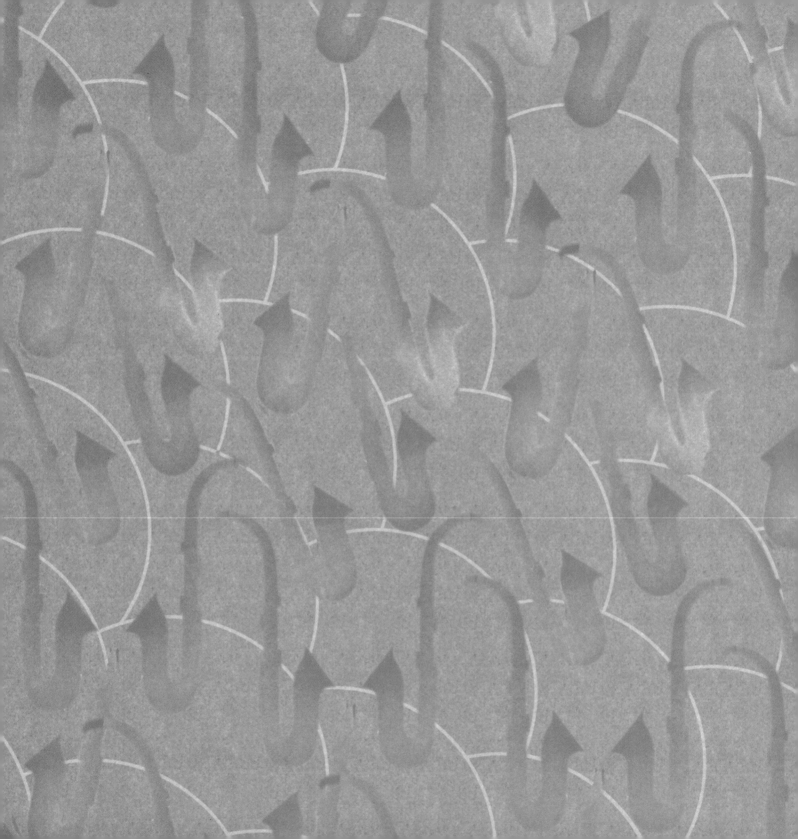

Celebrating the SAXOPHONE

PAUL LINDEMEYER

Design
RICK BEAULIEU

To John Wilkins —
All Best —
Paul Lindemeyer
3/99

HEARST BOOKS
NEW YORK

This book would not exist without the help of Dr. Paul Cohen of the Manhattan School of Music and Oberlin Conservatory — soloist, teacher, and the premier historian of the saxophone — who gave generously of his time, his archives, and his many rare instruments. Thanks, Paul.

It is the policy of William Morrow and Company, Inc., and its imprints and affiliates, recognizing the importance of preserving what has been written, to print the books we publish on acid-free paper, and we exert our best efforts to that end.

Library of Congress Cataloging-in-Publication Data
Lindemeyer, Paul.
Celebrating the saxophone / Paul Lindemeyer. — 1st ed.
    p.   cm.
Includes bibliographical references (p.   )
ISBN 0-688-13518-8
1. Saxophone — History.
I. Title.
ML975.L56 1996   95-46884
788.7'09 — dc20   CIP

Printed in Singapore
First Edition
1   2   3   4   5   6   7   8   9   1 0

Excerpt (p. 34) from *The Horn* by John Clellon Holmes.
Copyright © 1988 by John Clellon Holmes.
Reprinted with permission from Marlowe & Company.

Excerpt (p. 35) from *Ornette Coleman: A Harmolodic Life*
by John Litweiler. Copyright © 1992 by John Litweiler.
Reprinted with permission from William Morrow & Co.

Produced by SMALLWOOD & STEWART, INC., NEW YORK

CONTENTS

THE SAXOPHONE

THE SAXOPHONE PHENOMENON

THIS BOOK IS FOR ANYONE WHO HAS EVER fallen in love with the sound of a saxophone. ▣ From obscure origins in France one hundred and fifty years ago, the saxophone has evolved into an immensely popular instrument whose sound is immediately identifiable. The music of the twentieth century — especially jazz, of which the saxophone is the very soul — would be unthinkable without it. ▣ Play a sax and people respond. That's because, of all instruments, the saxophone reminds us most of the human voice. Its tones can be warm, cool, brilliant, tender, sultry-suave, or raw with energy. Young, old, or even tone-deaf: All immediately recognize the singular sound of the saxophone.

Meet Mickey Mouse, screen sax "cymbal," c. 1932, above. Even after the Roaring '20s, the saxophone was synonymous with fun and good times.

Bandleader Jimmy Dorsey was the solo saxman best known to the public in the '30s and '40s. Dance patrons would besiege him for his autograph on souvenir cards such as this one, left.

The big band era would never have happened without singing saxophones. No band was complete without three, four, or more. 20th Century-Fox captured the carefree elegance and excitement of the times in this musical number from *Sing, Baby, Sing* (1936), right.

8

THE SAXOPHONE'S INDIVIDUALITY has won over the world and made it the instrument of choice for solo expression. Until the '60s, when it gave way to the guitar, the saxophone was the best-selling instrument of them all. Like the guitar, it became a symbol. The sound or sight of a sax conjures vivid images: the fun and fancy of the roaring '20s; the sweetly swinging '30s; the brassy big band era of the '40s; '50s cool. The spirit of American individualism is incarnate in the urban hipster playing his plaintive sax in a smoke-filled club. We celebrate the saxophone because the saxophone so often celebrates us.

The sax made me buy it: Prestige Records scored a sizable success with bebopper James Moody's *I'm in the Mood for Love* in 1949. Singer King Pleasure added hip lyrics to the alto solo to make his own 1952 hit, *Moody Mood for Love.*

A poster for RKO Radio Pictures' *Syncopation* (1929), opposite, fairly sizzles with the vitality of Jazz Age music and dance.

Always important in jazz, the saxophone virtually took it over in the 1940s. So pervasive was the instrument that a *Jam Session,* below right, could be held with just one trumpet and many saxes.

The cool pure sound of Stan Getz, opposite in 1963, was crucial to the bossa-nova craze. His recordings with Antonio Carlos Jobim, João Gilberto, and others are classics.

oo long typed as a jazzy horn, the saxophone is only now

eginning to gain respect as a vehicle for classical and concert

music. Its use on the pop-rock scene was also limited until

elatively recently, due largely to its identification with

old-fashioned big bands. But once acknowledged, the

lexibility and range of 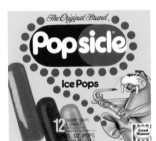 the sax family rapidly

made the instruments very popular. No doubt

he many voices of the sax will continue to

nspire and delight, and will make it a favorite of future

generations. That's because the music and lore of the saxophone

are rich and complex: so rich, that one book cannot tell it all. For

he real story, just listen — it is all around you.

You don't always hear them, but saxophones play a crucial support role in band music, smoothing the clash of brass and woodwind colors. School musicians find the sax fun and easy to learn, opposite.

Pops, the Popsicle Walrus, blows rings around the competition in the frozen treat case, left.

The soprano sax, long prized by jazz and classical musicians for its soaring lyricism, has found mass appeal with pop crossover artist Kenny G, below.

15

SAXOPHONE

ORIGINS

The basic saxophone design hasn't changed much since Adolphe Sax's day. All of his manufacture, the soprano, below, and the alto, tenor, and baritone, opposite from left to right, date from 1857 to 1861.

THE SAXOPHONE WAS THE BRAINCHILD of musical geniu. Adolphe Sax, of Belgium, whose many innovations in instrument making helped bring music into the Industria. Age. Around 1840, his obsession with brasses and woodwind. prompted him to develop an instrument that combined features of both. It would be a new voice unlike anything heard before and, in tribute to its inventor, would be called the saxophone. Sax was a giant in his time, a virtuoso clarinet soloist as well as the premier instrument manufacturer. But fame is fleeting, and when he died a century ago, he was impoverished, his contributions forgotten — except for a family of sleek brass/ reed horns whose time would soon come.

ANTOINE-JOSEPH SAX — known as Adolphe — was born in Dinant, Belgium, on November 6, 1814, the son of Charles-Joseph Sax, instrument maker to the king of The Netherlands. At 14, Adolphe Sax built his own clarinet of fine wood and soon was winning prizes at Europe's new industrial expositions. Sax was a rare young genius: an innovator whose hands were as facile as his mind.

When the Brussels Exposition denied his instruments a gold medal in 1841, Sax decided to seek his fortune elsewhere. He headed for Paris, penniless but rich in ideas. His favorite brainchild was a matched family of valved brasses. These "saxhorns" were the ancestors of the tubas, flügelhorns, and baritone horns heard in modern bands.

The saxophone may have been born when Sax, while puttering in his shop, fitted a bass clarinet mouthpiece and reed onto an ophicleide, a big bugle-type horn with keys instead of valves. At any rate, by 1842 he had made a bass saxophone, pitched in the key of C. It drew praise from Hector Berlioz, the renowned French composer, who transcribed some of his own

The Sax atelier in Paris was in its heyday in the 1850s, above.

A 1937 memorial tableau shows Sax playing for his patrons, left.

Some experiments were noble failures. Sax's multi-bell valve trombone, below, played in fine tune but was difficult to manipulate.

music for a demonstration concert with chamber winds on February 3, 1844, the first time a saxophone was heard in public, with Sax himself as soloist.

The saxhorns and saxophones attracted the attention of the French Army, who gave Sax the exclusive contract to outfit their bands. Established music firms couldn't compete with his superior craftsmanship and modern production methods, so they organized to ruin him. It was claimed he had stolen the saxophone idea, but the charge did not hold up in court. Sax patented his saxophones, by now a whole family, on March 20, 1846.

But even his important friends couldn't protect the instrument maker from the jealousy of a whole industry, which paid musicians to boycott Sax's products. Other problems ensued. After the 1860s, when his patents expired, anyone could copy Sax's instruments. Deprived of revenues from his inventions, Sax slipped back into poverty. In 1870, his Army contracts were canceled, and his factory went under. Bankrupt, he survived as a bandmaster at the Paris Opera until his death at 79 on February 4, 1894.

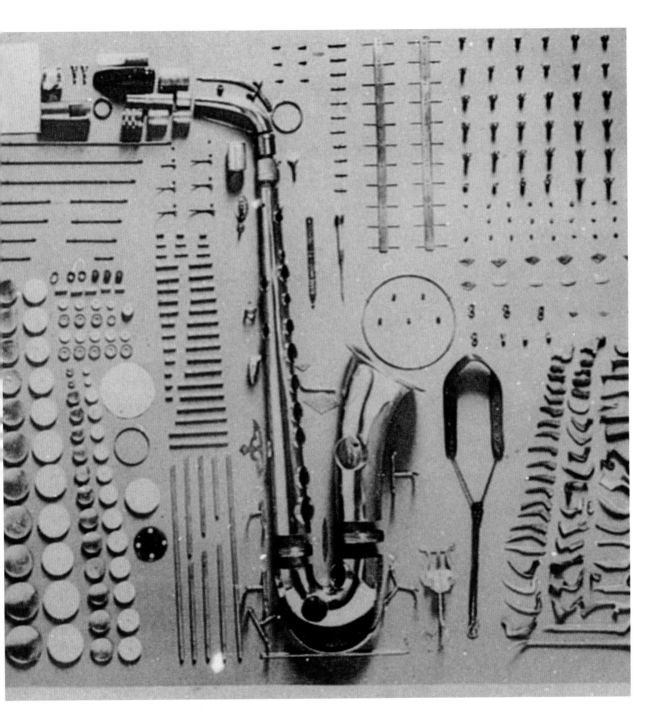

At left, an exploded view of the 1930 Conn 6M alto sax shows 510 individual parts, including leather pads and metal keycups (lower left), the key rods surrounding them, key mounting posts (upper right), and key ribs and touchpieces (lower right). The 1930 alto cost $100 in bare brass, $135 in satin silver, and $250 in gold. Depending on make, a professional alto can run from $1,500 to $2,500 (and up!) today.

The ophicleide, above, a brass bass of the early 19th century, was a predecessor of the sax. Its covered keys, rendered obsolete on brasses by piston valves, are very similar to those of a saxophone.

Colonel C. G. Conn built the world's largest band-instrument factory in Elkhart, Indiana. He also published newspapers and served in Congress. In 1888, Conn made the first American saxophones. By the 1920s, the horns made up 75% of the company's output. Conn went out of business in the 1960s.

F. A. (Gus) Buescher was a Conn craftsman before founding his own company in Elkhart in 1895. Buescher pioneered promoting sax sales with colorful ad campaigns. The Buescher True-Tone, Aristocrat, and 400 were favorites with musicians before the line was sold to Selmer in 1960.

Henri Selmer started as a clarinet virtuoso and maker of fine woodwinds. His Paris company only began manfacturing saxophones in 1922 but soon led the way in quality. The Mark VIs of 1954–73 were renowned for their fine tone and response and today are valuable collectibles.

EARLY SAXOPHONES WERE all French: Evette-Schaeffer and Buffet-Crampon were the best-known makers. The American passion for bands eventually gave rise to the "Music City" of Elkhart, Indiana, where a U.S. industry flourished from the 1880s to the 1960s. Elkhart boasted dozens of music firms, with Conn, Buescher, and Martin the giants. Other notable manufacturers included H. N. White's King brand, from Cleveland, and the Frank Holton Company, of Elkhorn, Wisconsin.

The 1930s brought low-priced student instruments — King's Cleveland, Selmer's Bundy — but industry consolidations in the 1950s and 1960s spelled the end of an era. L.A. Sax, an Illinois outfit, still makes saxes in the U.S., but today the saxophone scene is increasingly international. Japan's Yamaha and Yanagisawa and Germany's Julius Keilwerth are renowned makers, while Selmer and Buffet perpetuate France's love affair with the instrument. The Czech Amati, the Italian Grassi and Romeo Orsi, along with several off-price Far Eastern brands, also compete in today's saxophone market.

Saxophones have always been built to tolerances of thousandths of an inch. Nowadays, computer design allows for finer engineering and instruments that are more consistent in intonation and response than their predecessors.

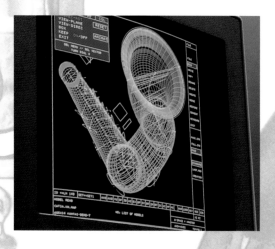

Even today, the first steps in manufacturing are relatively crude. High-quality sheet brass is hammered on an anvil into a rough, bell-like shape.

The saxophone bell is machine-spun into precisely the right shape and dimensions. It is then highly polished and coated with clear or gold lacquer before the maker's distinctive designs are hand-engraved.

The complicated key system is installed last. The highest-quality sax keys are power-forged to precise dimensions rather than made in molds. Tone-hole rims are likewise power-drawn from the body tube.

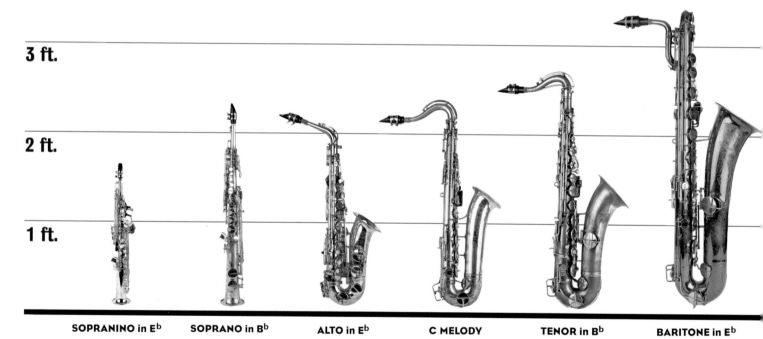

6 ft.

5 ft.

4 ft.

3 ft.

2 ft.

1 ft.

SOPRANINO in E♭	**SOPRANO in B♭**	**ALTO in E♭**	**C MELODY**	**TENOR in B♭**	**BARITONE in E♭**
Selmer (Paris) Super Action 80 Series II, 1993	Selmer (Paris) Model 26, in gold plate, 1929	Selmer (Paris) Mark VI, 1965	Selmer (Paris) Model 22, 1924	Conn 10M "Chu Berry", in silver plate with gold keys, 1928	Buescher Aristocrat, 1933

THE SAXOPHONE FAMILY spans nearly seven octaves, yet only the alto, soprano, tenor, and baritone models are widely played.

The most popular saxophone is the rich, lyrical alto, the horn most beginners learn and the keystone of the classical solo repertory. In solo jazz and rock, the alto is important, too, but less so than the more powerful tenor.

Concert and jazz soloists love the penetrating soprano, despite its tricky intonation (the piping little sopranino is more difficult yet). The baritone adds ensemble "bottom" and solo color, and has largely pushed aside the majestic but unwieldy bass.

Bass saxes are still made on special order. The contrabass is as rare as it is impractical, but its organlike low tones are unforgettable. The C melody and C soprano, made for home use with vocal music, vanished from production after the 1920s.

BASS in B♭

Conn 14M, with key
range to high F, 1930

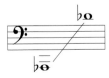

CONTRABASS in E♭

Evette-Schaeffer,
built by Buffet-
Crampon, c. 1920

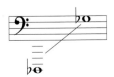

**WRITTEN RANGE of
ALL SAXOPHONES**

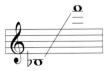

VARIATIONS ON THE THEME

ONE-HANDED TENOR, 1918

Conn customized this instrument for a novelty act that required the player to blow two saxophones at once. (The right hand did all the work.) In the '60s, Rahsaan Roland Kirk would use similarly modified horns, playing three at a time.

MEZZO-SOPRANO in F, 1928

Conn's "new" model was really Adolphe Sax's idea: an alto in F, to play French horn or English horn parts. But the sax mania had peaked by 1925 and the idea didn't catch on. Most models ended up on the scrap pile.

LOOMIS Double Resonance ALTO, 1920

American engineer Allen Loomis redesigned the saxophone for better tone, tune, and response, including a range to low A. But plain old saxes were selling just fine. Only six prototypes were ever built.

IN BROAD TECHNICAL TERMS, a saxophone is an instrument with a single-reed mouthpiece like that of a clarinet, covered keys operated by levers, and a conical tube that widens from mouthpiece to bell.

The combination of single reed and conical tube is what makes the saxophone unique. Woodwinds make use of the harmonic phenomenon of overblowing: You get a higher note out of the same length of tube by exerting greater lip pressure or by opening a small octave key. A woodwind instrument with uniform diameter tubing, like the clarinet, will overblow to a note an octave and a fifth higher: C in the lower octave to G above. Conical-tube winds speak in simple octaves, making for easier learning and fingering.

Saxophones haven't changed much in 150 years, a tribute to the elegance and simplicity of Sax's original design. Improvements have made them easier to play and increased their range. The original two octave keys, which were tricky to manipulate, gave way to one automatic key, which was invented in 1887. The original range of low B to high F was extended to low B-flat sometime early in this century. Today, baritones typically reach low A, and sopranos, altos, and tenors often have high F-sharp attachments.

27

GRAFTON PLASTIC ALTO, 1950s

The English-made Grafton acrylic sax had a wonderful sound but wasn't durable. Ornette Coleman wore out several. Charlie Parker's model recently sold for more than $200,000.

CONN-O-SAX in F, 1928

This marked another futile attempt by the industry leader to market a new horn. Modeled on the orchestra heckelphone, the Conn-o-sax had extra high F-sharp and G keys.

The saxophonist's search for the perfect mouthpiece never ends. Some swear by established brands such as Brilhart (left) or Otto Link (third from left). A good piece is generally hard rubber or metal but can also be made of plastic, glass, or wood. Rubber gives a warmer tone, while metal affords more volume and bite.

THE SAXOPHONE WAS FIRST USED IN MILITARY BANDS, where it was a voice of compromise between blasting brass and piping clarinets. In the late nineteenth century, John Philip Sousa adopted the sax, along with other distinguished bandmasters such as Patrick Gilmore and Pat Conway. They composed mostly marches, but their bands' repertoires ranged from operatic favorites to ragtime. Then came the sax explosion of this century. Here was an instrument whose warm, humanlike tonality had few limits. As the decades progressed, it would seem the saxophone had been created to express the restless energy of modern America.

The Six Brown Brothers, opposite, were the instrument's great popularizers in ragtime vaudeville, c. 1915.

29

SAXOPHONES HAD BEEN mainstays in military bands ever since Adolphe Sax won his French Army contract in 1845. Sax himself taught at the Paris Conservatory until the Franco-Prussian War of 1870 suspended classes. By then, clarinet professors at various schools in France, Belgium, and Switzerland gave saxophone instruction. Much early music was penned by Jean-Baptiste Singelée, who wrote solos and, in 1857, the first important quartet.

But outside French-speaking Europe, the saxophone was slow to gain acceptance. A bass saxophone part was written for a French opera as early as 1844, but saxophones were heard only occasionally in opera houses. The most familiar example is the alto solo in Georges Bizet's 1872 opera *L'Arlesienne*.

Meanwhile, in New York City, Americans had gotten their first taste of the saxophone when Louis Jullien's French band played there in 1853. W. H. Fry wrote a soprano part into his *Santa Claus Symphony* in 1853, and Harvey Dodworth included a tenor sax in his band in Central Park in the 1860s.

The first star saxophonist was Edouard Lefèbre (1834–1911), a French

Edouard Lefèbre (second from right) was the first great saxophone virtuoso. He traveled worldwide with bands and with his Conn Wonder Quartet, shown here in 1901.

This 1919 song, below, was one of many inspired by the sax.

altoist who played in Patrick Gilmore's band from 1873 to 1892, then became a traveling teacher and artist for the C. G. Conn Company. Bands provided a showcase for new musical talents and trends. Central to civilian and military life, bands entertained with light classics, transcriptions of orchestral works, and, of course, marches. Most were homegrown, formed from towns-people playing horns and drums of Civil War vintage. But the era of the professional musician was beginning. Musically trained leaders and sidemen, many foreign born, began to tour. The alto saxophone gained an identity as a solo instrument, alongside the cornet, trombone, and other winds.

Band soloists needed exquisite tone and technique. H. Benne Henton (1867–1938), alto saxophonist with the bands of John Philip Sousa and Pat Conway, had both. Recordings reveal Henton to have been breathtakingly fast, expressive, and capable of notes an octave or more above the key range. This altissimo register is now widespread in classical and jazz saxophoning.

Sousa's band, begun in 1892, was the most famous ensemble of its kind.

Among Sousa's other fine sax soloists was Belgian Jean Moeremans. One of the first saxophonists to make records, Moeremans appeared on disc labels as early as 1897 and had a hit with *Carnival*

in Venice in 1904. It was a typical turn-of-the-century sax solo, an old chestnut tricked up with showy variations.

As the sax grew in popularity, so did its numbers. Colonel C. G. Conn, who became America's number-one

music manufacturer, was the first to mass-produce instruments, such as his "Wonder" saxes, which sold for less than comparable French products of the same quality.

The saxophones' fame and popularity were spreading fast. They could now be heard everywhere from Portugal to Imperial Russia, except England and Germany, whose musical traditions had little use for this new-fangled contraption.

Saxophones were still rare in non-band music. Richard Strauss's *Domestic Symphony* (1902) included a quartet in a strictly ensemble role. But it was a woman who was responsible for a major breakthrough in the use of the saxophone, especially in America. Elise Boyer Hall (1853–1924) took up the saxophone while recovering from typhoid fever. At salon evenings, resplendent in a pink gown, Mrs. Hall performed pieces she had commissioned from French composers. Claude Debussy's *Rhapsody* for alto saxophone and chamber orchestra was a Hall commission. Begun in 1903 and orchestrated posthumously, it is the composer's only work for saxophone.

Elise Boyer Hall, above, introduced the saxophone to Boston society in the early 1900s. She commissioned music for it as well; the manuscripts reside at the New England Conservatory.

Center, the breathtaking cadenza from Benne Henton's *Eleven O'Clock Fantasy*, 1911.

Community bands were slower to adopt saxophones than their professional cousins. Early converts were the New York City Police Band of 1908, bottom left.

NEW YORK CITY POLICE BAND.

THE TWENTIETH CENTURY has often been called the "American Century," an appellation perhaps most apt in the field of popular music. The sounds of America in the 1900s provided the backdrop to a national coming of age: Our dynamic young society hummed to the rhythms of bustling cities and the immigrants who flocked to them. Ragtime, an African-American music, had overtaken our hearts and made them beat with syncopated joy. And in New York City's Tin Pan Alley, immigrant songwriters such as Irving Berlin were writing the tunes the whole world would soon be whistling.

In cities and towns, traveling vaudeville troupes were in their heyday.

Groups such as the Darling Four, left, flourished in vaudeville, but women remained outsiders in most of the music profession.

Jazz adopted the sax due to popular demand. By 1919, the Original Dixieland Jazz Band, below, added the instrument so many had come to love in dance orchestras.

Sax groups sang out their jaunty harmonies through the teens and '20s. The Army's Rainbow Division sextet, above, played all through France in 1918.

It was these companies' never-ending search for something novel that led them, around 1910, to incorporate solo and ensemble saxophone playing into their acts. The public was soon to follow in their footsteps.

The sax family of instruments was a natural for choirs — and it was easy to learn! The Six Brown Brothers, led by Tom Brown, began playing their music on Broadway and recorded on the Victor label in 1913. Their two alto, tenor, two baritone, and bass saxes piped out ragtime specialties like *Down Home Rag, Bull Frog Blues,* and *Darktown Strutters' Ball.*

This music, though jaunty, was simple and did not take full advantage

of the instruments' capabilities. But even so, to the public the Browns were utterly fascinating. The saxophone's striking resemblance to the human voice was having a mesmerizing effect.

Sax-tets of all sizes appeared in the teens, often with costume themes. There were Saxophone Highlanders, Saxophone Hussars, and an impressive array of female troupes.

Musicians in the new dance orchestras also began adopting the sax. By 1914, some six thousand new saxophones were being sold per year in America. Editor D. A. McDonald of *Dominant Magazine* praised "its beautiful, expressive voice, its facility of execution in all keys, its flexibility of tone . . . and its particular charm as a solo instrument." No instrument, he wrote, had a more promising future.

The traveling Chautauqua tent shows, which presented high-toned "family entertainments," eschewed Tin Pan Alley music, but they did feature Smith and Holmes's Apollo Quartet. Their arrangements of light concert favorites, such as Schubert's *Serenade,* Liszt's *Second Hungarian Rhapsody,* and the *Quartet* from Verdi's

Rudy Wiedoeft. His C melody, and virtuoso technique, made him king of the saxophone in the teens and '20s.

Among Wiedoeft's many compositions was the 1919 *Saxophone Blues.*

opera *Rigoletto*, were the first widely published sax-quartet pieces.

Today, only a few remember the saxophone's first great popularizer. The satin-silver tone and lightning-fast technique of Rudy Wiedoeft (1893–1940) once made him the most imitated and admired of instrumental musicians. A recording and stage artist from 1917 on, he was the first saxophone soloist most people ever heard.

Because so little original music existed, Wiedoeft transcribed old favorites such as Brahms's *Hungarian Dance.* He also composed his own demanding solo pieces, including ornate waltzes like *Valse Erica* and *Valse Vanité,* as well as raggy novelties with a million notes a minute like *Saxophobia, Saxema, Saxarella,* and *Sax-O-Phun.* His unique mix of artistry and sentimentality captured listeners and inspired countless imitators.

It was Rudy Wiedoeft and the Six Brown Brothers who gave the saxophone a foothold in popular music in the teens of this century. And it was they who paved the way for its astonishing explosion in popularity in the next decade: the sax-crazy 1920s.

He considered the polished keys and the catsup-colored neck of the tenor saxophone which, two years earlier, had cost him $175 on Sixth Avenue, becoming his after an hour of careful scales and haggling and of the gradual ease which comes to a man's fingers when they lose their natural suspicion of an instrument or a machine which is not their own, but must be made to respond like some sinewy, indifferent horse, not reluctant to be owned but simply beautiful in its blooded ignorance of ownership. . . . To Walden the saxophone was, at once, his key to the world in which he found himself, and the way by which that world was rendered

THE QUOTABLE SAXOPHONE

impotent to brand him either failure or madman or Negro or saint. But then sometimes on the smoky stand, between solos, he hung it from his swinging shoulder like one bright, golden wing, and waited for his time.

~ **JOHN CLELLON HOLMES, "THE HORN" (1953)**

I have never heard anything so beautiful.

~ **GIOACCHINO ROSSINI**

An unhindered technique, expressive range, and directness of speech that has its equal only in the modern flute.

~ **PAUL HINDEMITH**

The tenor's got that thing, that honk, you can get to people with it. Sometimes you can be playing that tenor and I'm telling you, the people want to jump across the rail.

35

~ **ORNETTE COLEMAN**

That muddy instrument.

~ **CLAUDE DEBUSSY**

I know how to write for the saxophones, but I don't know how to conduct them! They make me nervous!

~ **VICTOR HERBERT**

THE SAXOPHO

By the '20s, the young century had found its own unique voice in the saxophone. This was a jazz age, a decade when a fast-stepping world danced to America's tune: the music of radio, records, and Tin Pan Alley. A "moaning" saxophone came to connote the  youth culture of fun, fads, and frivolity. A sax took pride of place alongside the parlor piano in many a home. ▣ The '20s craze eventually faded. But saxophones had become as common and familiar to Americans as telephones. The '30s, '40s, and '50s saw them at the fore, inspiring a parade of solo geniuses who would forever change the sound of modern American music. The great saxophone era was upon us.

Paul Whiteman and his orchestra, opposite, go national over the NBC network in 1932.

The Whiteman Sax-Soc-Tette, previous pages, was a popular feature with the band in the late '30s.

39

As 1920 DAWNED, Rudy Wiedoeft and the concert-band movement were still the biggest influences on young saxophone players. But that was changing as jazz and, more specifically, the dance orchestra, rose to popularity.

Amazingly, in the beginning, there were no saxophones in jazz. In its earliest days in New Orleans, the trumpet, trombone, and clarinet — as in the Original Dixieland Jazz Band — wove together intricate, improvisational music. It took Sidney Bechet, a clarinet man from New Orleans, to get the idea to improvise jazz solos on a saxophone. Bechet became the greatest player of the soprano sax in jazz history. Although Coleman Hawkins's tenor would inspire more musicians, Bechet

first proved the sax as a jazz instrument.

There was jazz, the African-American music derived from ragtime and the blues, and then there was jazz as the white public knew it, which could be any rhythm ditty played for dancing. And people were dancing as never before. Ballrooms were newly popular, featuring six-to-eight-piece dance orchestras playing written arrangements. The groups sought sweetness, freshness, and versatility. Saxophones had all that. Saxes mixed beautifully with brass and carried further than clarinets or violins. Clarinetists found them easy to double on, and since all saxes played the same, one could add different-sized horns for even more color. Saxophones were an immediate hit, and dance musicians

Paul Whiteman, with his 1920 orchestra on sheet music for their big hit, *Wang-Wang Blues*, above, is largely credited with the birth of the big band.

1920s sax sections, left, took "doubling" to extremes not seen again until the free-jazz movement of the 1960s.

who shunned them soon found themselves hurting for jobs.

Isham Jones (1894–1956), who penned such hit songs as *It Had to Be You,* played tenor with his band as early as 1915, and Paul Whiteman's first orchestra, in 1919, carried a two-alto sax section. Whiteman, billed as "King of Jazz," would become *the* popular bandleader of the '20s. By 1925, big bands of ten pieces standardized on two altos and a tenor, pitched alongside the brass of two trumpets and a trombone. Whiteman mounted a much larger ensemble, whose sax team doubled in clarinets, flutes, and double-reeds for richly scored "concert pop" sounds: most memorably, George Gershwin's *Rhapsody in Blue.* Indeed, Jaap Kool's 1930 book, *The Saxophone,* proclaimed that the best saxophone playing in all of music was to be heard in Whiteman's band. Particularly notable was the section's subtle use of the vibrato, which many less-accomplished musicians overemphasized.

Kool, a Dutch musicologist, knew popular music but not the real jazz. He never mentioned Fletcher Henderson's orchestra, which, starting in 1924,

SIDNEY BECHET
FIRST SAXOPHONE OF JAZZ

Sidney Bechet of New Orleans (1897–1959) made the soprano saxophone his personal voice, at once metallic and elastic, earthy and electric. Key to his style was an intense, wide vibrato — carried over from the clarinet, which he never abandoned — and an expressive throat "growl" used only on saxophone.

Taking up soprano in 1920 during a European tour, Bechet played alongside young Louis Armstrong in Clarence Williams's Blue Five recording group in 1924–25 (*Complete Sessions,* EPM, France). In 1932, he started his own short-lived band, The New Orleans Feetwarmers, but spent most of the '30s as star soloist in Noble Sissle's globe-trotting big band, where he doubled baritone and bass sax in the ensemble.

The Dixieland revival of the 1940s revitalized Bechet's career as a solo attraction (*The Bluebird Sessions,* Bluebird). In 1949, he relocated to France, where he was a beloved figure on the pop music charts and even earned a gold record.

Sidney taught both Johnny Hodges, of the Ellington band, and Bob Wilber, a leader in the traditional jazz revival movement. But the soprano sax has seen wide use only in modern jazz, thanks to the innovations of Steve Lacy and John Coltrane.

Frank Trumbauer, left, was the only great jazzman to make a specialty of the C melody sax, so popular with amateur players.

Adrian Rollini, right, champion of the bass saxophone, transformed the slow, oafish instrument into a solo powerhouse.

42

Jimmy Dorsey, left, one of the earliest hot jazz alto players to make an impact in the '20s, went on to fame with his own big band.

combined the two, blending hot solos into exciting, rhythmic dance music. Henderson featured the arrangements and alto sax of Don Redman (1900–64), a lithe player who took a backseat as soloist to trumpeter Louis Armstrong and tenor-sax virtuoso Coleman Hawkins. "Hawk" brought incredible energy and imagination to this polite ballad saxophone, becoming the single most important saxophone stylist in jazz until the arrival on the scene of Charlie Parker in the 1940s.

Hawkins helped make the tenor

e correct solo sax in jazz. The alto was
sed mostly for straight melody; the
thers strictly for effects. Still, the cross-
reeding of jazz and dance music gave
se to solo talent on every type of sax.

Early on, most of the best-known
players were white. Jimmy Dorsey
(1904–57) was a clarinet and alto star
whose peerless technique, rich tone,
and distinctive rapid vibrato made him
a hot commodity on radio and recordings, along with his trombonist brother,
Tommy Dorsey. When the 1930s
came, both enjoyed tremendous success
as bandleaders. Like Jimmy Dorsey,
Benny Goodman and Artie Shaw
played alto in many a band section
before their days of fame.

Frank Trumbauer (1901–56)
adapted hot jazz to the C melody
saxophone. "Tram" used the flexibility
of the C sax to play jazz with wit,
humor, and a cool tone that inspired
Lester Young and, through him, Stan
Getz. Like Rudy Wiedoeft, he was
capable of breathtaking speed and technique, displayed in modernistic '30s
pieces like *Sun Spots, Meteor,* and
Eclipse. Unfortunately, the style and the
C melody itself fell from favor by 1940.

COLEMAN HAWKINS
BODY AND SOUL OF THE TENOR SAX

Coleman Hawkins (1904–69) was the first to establish a jazz voice for the tenor saxophone. Hawk developed his sound in Fletcher Henderson's orches-tra, below, from 1923 to 1934, taking full advantage of the harmonic palette by phrasing in arpeggios with a searing, pene-trating tone and a power and drive unequaled up to that time (*Fletcher Henderson,* Classics). The sound was creat-ed by his use of a hard reed and open-tipped metal mouth-piece, equipment that became the favored setup for jazz players.
   From 1934 to 1939, Hawkins was the first of many sax-ophonists to go over-seas as a solo

virtuoso. Back home, he pioneered the extended jazz solo with his recording *Body and Soul* (*Body and Soul*, Bluebird). This three-minute improvisation is still the most studied and admired of all

saxophone solos.
   Hawkins kept up with changing fashions in postwar jazz (*The Hawk Flies High*, Prestige), but never compromised his basic swing identity. Though today's fashion is to follow more recent players, Hawk's music is time-less. As Thelonious Monk said, "No one can pick up a tenor saxophone without playing some of him."

The bass saxophone, heard in the '20s as a solo voice or as a substitute for the tuba in rhythm sections, briefly came to prominence through Adrian Rollini (1903–56). A nightclub owner and recording artist, Rollini overcame the instrument's "potatoey" tone and sluggish execution to produce high-powered rhythmic solos after the manner of Coleman Hawkins's tenor. But pop bands never really made a place for such a big sound, and Rollini was forced to give up the bass sax, which surfaced again in the Dixieland revival groups of the '40s and '50s.

Of course, '20s jazz bands were not the only forum for saxophone musicians. Rudy Wiedoeft had inspired a plethora of virtuosi who inhabited the now-forgotten world between pop and light classics. Merle Johnston's Quartet and Clyde Doerr's Sextet offered pleasing styles of dance music that never quite caught on. Bennie Krueger, the clown of the saxophone, could make the instrument "laugh," "cry," and even "hiccup." Andy Sannella was famed both as an alto soloist and steel guitarist. And Kathryn Thompson, director of a private sax

school, was the only woman saxophonist who, prior to the '60s, would gain public acceptance.

With so much of a saxophone flavor to the times, it was inevitable that the horn would get attention from "legitimate" composers of a modernist bent, even if stuffy traditionalists sneered at its razzmatazz associations. Besides Gershwin's orchestral pieces and Maurice Ravel's 1928 *Bolero*,

saxophones figure prominently in 1920s chamber and symphonic works by Béla Bartok (*The Wooden Prince*), Aaron Copland (*Piano Concerto* and *Symphony No. 1*), Darius Milhaud, Percy Grainger, Paul Hindemith, and many others. And as 1930 approached, a few concert recitalists began to devote themselves exclusively to the saxophone, setting the stage for a classical solo tradition that flourishes today.

The giddy '20s pop culture put the sax on top of the world — right along with the 1927 champion New York Yankees. Lou Gehrig reacts to Babe Ruth's agonizing alto in a very familiar way. Ruth could hit baseballs but notes were another thing.

Saxo-Mania was exactly the word for the tooting frenzy. This and many other novelty airs filled the decade with ricky-ticky rhythms.

44

SELLING THE SAXOPHONE

THE PLAY-AT-HOME CRAZE

The American '20s was a giddy, fad-happy time of flappers, flivvers, and flagpole-sitters. Not so well remembered is the tremendous boom in amateur saxophone playing — a consumer music frenzy unequaled until the guitar mania of the '60s.

Before radio took over our home entertainment needs, parlor pianos and sing-alongs were a cherished part of American life. Into this cozy setting now came the C melody sax, made especially for playing popular vocal music. Although expensive to buy — a C melody might cost $60 or $70 when a cornet or banjo could be yours for $15 — a saxophone was fun and fashionable. "Popularity Plus!" was

the theme of the Buescher Company's campaign, which promised "the glad hand of welcome everywhere."

The ease of getting started was key to the craze. With the free fingering chart, a beginner could squeak out the scale before a novice violinist had learned to pull a bow. (One book even called itself the *Five-Minute Saxophone Course!*) And the horn was perfect for all ages, stressed its makers, requiring no extreme effort for young or old.

The peak years were 1923 and 1924, when 100,000 saxophones a year were made, most in the giant music factories of Elkhart, Indiana. The great demand resulted in "stenciling," or marketing the same models under different names. A Conn or Martin sax might have carried the Lyon & Healy engraving, while a Buescher might have been called a Wurlitzer, a Carl Fischer, or even a Selmer — until the Paris atelier began producing its own saxophone in 1922.

"Why does not every musical person play the saxophone?" wondered musicologist Jaap Kool, pointing out that a good standard of playing could be had in a year or two. But few of the young upstarts dazzled by the showy virtuosity of Rudy Wiedoeft had the patience to really *learn* the horn — preferring, as teacher Kathryn Thompson put it, to "twist around on one foot and 'honk' a few wavy, accordion-pleated tones that sound more like a bleating lamb than a musical instrument."

Bad sax playing didn't do justice to the instrument's capabilities. And it did little to help the horn's image with those who prided themselves on their love of "good music."

By 1927, sales were falling and thousands of C melodies were headed for hall closets and pawnshops. But the saxophone itself was anything but a fad. Its unique sound and rare expressiveness assured that its place in music had been won for good.

When the 1930s began, saxophones were here to stay. The heady jazz age that had adopted the sound of the sax as its siren call was over by 1930. But the horn had proved itself too musical to be just a fad. Saxophones had survived the heyday and slow death of vaudeville and were now heard in every theater pit and radio studio, and on every football field and ballroom stand.

The early 1930s saw further progress in the concert halls. Several saxophone artists tried their fortunes as classical recitalists. Three virtuosi — Sigurd Raschèr in Germany, Marcel Mule in France, and Cecil Leeson in America — began to build a repertory and a tradition for the solo alto. Mule did much to further the sax quartet as a chamber ensemble. In the years to come, the achievements and musicianship of Raschèr, Mule, and Leeson would win them a rightful place alongside the Heifetzes, Horowitzes, and Rubinsteins. Even if they never did become such household names, they brought the instrument more well-deserved respect and admiration than ever before. The days of snide sax jokes were over, never to return.

The '30s brought the Great Depression and with it a marked change in public taste. Hard times demanded music that was simple and safe. Radio singers and their sentimental ballads took center stage as dance bands slowed their tempo to a tasteful crawl. Hot jazz continued to evolve in African-American circles, but its white audience disappeared. Would the saxophone, that jazzy instrument, fade from the pop scene too?

Hardly. "Sweet bands," a popular musical trend that made white dance music more romantic than ever, relied on sax harmony as never before. The pioneers were Guy Lombardo's Royal Canadians, founded in 1928 as the first pop group with a distinctive saxophone section sound. Almost too soft and lilting, with exaggerated vibrato and phrasing, the sax trio was styled by Guy's alto-playing brother, Carmen Lombardo (1904–71). The Lombardos' success once again showed the power of sax music to reach the public. Dozens of bands imitated their stylized sound. Another model was Freddy Martin (1908–83), whose deep-toned sax section was made up of three tenors

Benny Goodman poses with his trailblazing orchestra of 1935, above, the model for many more in the swing era. A former section alto player, Goodman forsook saxophones entirely as a superstar clarinet soloist.

Duke Ellington's sax team, below, one of the greatest,

was led by Otto Hardwicke (left). Johnny Hodges (right) and Harry Carney (second from left) were tops on alto and baritone for decades. Barney Bigard (second from right) played tenor in the ensemble but soloed only on clarinet. Ellington didn't have a tenor soloist until Ben Webster

in 1940; his was the only major orchestra without one.

Dancing was what it was about in the '30s, opposite. The public craved the lush reed harmony in big bands. These collegians, grooving to Glenn Miller in 1939, enjoyed his clarinet-led sax team and the solos of tenor Tex Beneke.

including his own. Martin was the inspiration for "tenor bands," which would croon away in hotel and club rooms even into the '60s.

More sophisticated early '30s sounds included the Hal Kemp orchestra, whose sax trio stepped smartly through complicated sixteenth-note passages. Ben Bernie's band spotted an amazing alto technician, Dick Stabile (1909–80), who wrote a widely read saxophone advice column for *Metronome* magazine. And in London in 1931, Ray Noble's band enriched the customary trio of two altos and a tenor with a thrilling deep baritone, inspired no doubt by the use of the instrument by Duke Ellington's orchestra.

From 1928 until his death in 1974, Ellington and his orchestra were at the forefront of creative jazz. Among Ellington's gifts was his fine ear for solo talents, including some of the greatest musicians ever to pick up a saxophone. The baritone sax was key to his special section sound, and Harry Carney (1910–74) was his longtime baritone specialist. Carney's warm, huge sound and easy phrasing in every register made him the perfect anchor and bottom

48

voice of a four-piece reed section. He was the instrument's most prominent soloist until well into the '40s, and it was impossible to imagine the Ellington band without him. Soon after Ellington passed on, Carney too was gone.

Another Ellington veteran was Johnny Hodges (1907–70), considered for many years the most creative player of the alto saxophone. Taught soprano by Sidney Bechet, "Jeep" played that instrument as well. But his alto playing was his great contribution. He was one of the few 1930s saxophonists to overcome the stereotype of the alto as strictly a section lead, leaving that work to the excellent Otto Hardwicke. Hodges combined an utterly pure, luminous tone with tangy, blues-tinged phrasing and a miraculous way of bending a note up to pitch, a technique the flexible saxophone lends itself to very well. As the resident romantic in Ellington's stable of stars, Hodges rendered powerfully tender themes like *Warm Valley* and *Passion Flower*, tunes he made his own. Most influenced by the Hodges style were Benny Carter, Willie Smith, and Charlie Barnet. Charlie Parker said of

The saxophonist's saxophonist is Benny Carter, right. His flowingly lyrical alto sound has graced jazz for seven decades.

im: "He can *sing* with the horn! He's a beautiful person."

By 1934, Prohibition had been repealed and FDR's New Deal was giving America a new optimism. Real jazz began to meet enthusiastic audiences, setting the stage for what we know as swing music. During the swing era, which lasted until about 1945, the dynamic big band sound gave rise to a new generation of stars. Among these household names — Benny Goodman, Artie Shaw, and Count Basie — one could find Charlie Barnet (1913–91), the sax-blowing matinée idol and the only well-known soloist to play both alto and tenor.

The dance music of a previous era, as exemplified by the bands of Paul Whiteman, Guy Lombardo, and Hal Kemp, continued to draw audiences but blazed few new trails. Whiteman, though, *did* experiment in the late '30s with a "Sax-Soc-Tette" (sax-octet), an updating of the old vaudeville idea with doublings in flutes and clarinets.

The swing craze really began with the success of Benny Goodman, whose band played the crisp, sparkling arrangements of Fletcher Henderson.

Swing rhythms were smoother and bands bigger, sporting five to seven brasses and four saxes — two altos and two tenors. By 1940, the sax quintet (adding one baritone) opened up new possibilities for harmony and sonority. This was the high point of the era, with some two hundred traveling name

bands, each with its suave row of sax-men swaying back and forth under the spotlights of ballrooms and clubs.

Some of the saxophonists who came to prominence in the '30s had been playing for a decade or more. By now, Coleman Hawkins was an international celebrity whose tenor mastery had been *the* influence in jazz sax. A Hawkins school had arisen with Ben Webster, Leon "Chu" Berry, and

Johnny Hodges (center) was for years the unchallenged king of jazz alto saxophone. Bud Freeman and Chu Berry (left and right) join him on tenors in a 1939 jam session.

Herschel Evans as Hawkins's best pupils.

Ben Webster (1909–73) was the first to emerge fully from the master's shadow. When Hawkins left Fletcher Henderson's band in 1934, it was Webster who took his place. By the time he joined Duke Ellington in 1940, he was his own man. Webster's famous solo in *Cotton Tail*, recorded with Ellington on RCA, featured scorching altissimo notes and a blues influence carried from his native Kansas City. His "fuzz tone," a breathy, furry edge to a rich tenor sound, added the new dimension of texture to saxophone esthetics. It was Webster who would inspire the Texas and rhythm & blues genres of solo sax. In the '50s and '60s, Webster smoothed over his sound to become the premier practitioner of jazz balladry. Ben Webster could make the simplest melody totally his own.

Chu Berry (1910–41) pioneered a slightly less powerful, more rhythmic version of Hawkins's style in the Fletcher Henderson and Cab Calloway orchestras. A car crash cut short his life, but Berry was key to the exciting tenor sounds of Georgie Auld, Tex Beneke, and Charlie Barnet. Also short-lived,

Herschel Evans (1909–39) proved an effective foil to the cool style of Lester Young in the Count Basie band. Other prominent disciples included Budd Johnson with Earl Hines's orchestra, Babe Russin and Vido Musso with Benny Goodman, and Dick Wilson with Andy Kirk.

A young tenor player had to be very sure of himself not to imitate the Hawkins style. One such maverick was Lester Young, a genius so ahead of his time that his real influence would not be felt for years. Another iconoclast was Bud Freeman (1906–91), whose primitive yet elegant sound first surfaced in the small groups of '20s Chicago jazz. Freeman's elemental growling phrases, spiced with strange, disjointed arpeggios, seemed to flow from the innovations of clarinetist Pee Wee Russell. Freeman was featured with the Tommy Dorsey orchestra and later was one of the few important saxophone players in Dixieland revival music. Melding the styles of Freeman and Hawkins into some very swinging playing was Eddie Miller (b. 1911), a fixture of the Bob Crosby orchestra and its satellite group, the Bob Cats.

50

Attracting attention with his new band in 1933 was alto saxophonist Benny Carter (b. 1907). His fluent and insightful solos combine Hodges's lessons in tone with his own quick melodic invention. The versatile Carter has doubled as trumpeter and composer-arranger of classic jazz pieces dating back to his 1933 band. *Symphony in Riffs*, the alto feature *Melancholy Lullaby*, and *Lonesome Nights* are but a few of his

Ben Webster broke through as a major tenor voice in the early '40s. His gutsy style would influence even more young players than Coleman Hawkins's as time went on.

compositions. Carter spent much of the '30s in Europe as a soloist and arranger. Back home, he led great bands, wrote movie scores, and released two acclaimed sax ensemble albums on the Impulse! label. Fellow altoman David Sanborn has called him "the consummate musician . . . He represents what American music is all about."

In the tradition of Carter and Jimmy Dorsey were the great lead altomen Toots Mondello (1910–91) and Hilton Jefferson (1903–68). Though the alto was kept in its place by published arrangements giving solos only to tenors and clarinets, Mondello and Jefferson made the most of their few solo spots. Arnold Brilhart (b. 1904), a radio sideman, stuck to section work and was much in demand. He left performing to design and merchandise sax mouthpieces and reeds. Most featured of the lead men was Willie Smith (1910–67), a Johnny Hodges-like player who headed Jimmie Lunceford's marvelous section through intricate and difficult arrangements. Joe Thomas's tenor solos also energized the Lunceford band, remembered as one of the most musical and showmanly groups of the 1930s.

THE CLASSICAL SAXOPHONE

FOUNDERS OF A TRADITION

The 1930s saw the beginning of a musical movement that has yet to reach the mass audience: the performance of classical solo and ensemble music for the saxophone. By 1950, the bedrock of the instrument's concert repertory was in place, inspired by three virtuosi and teachers.

Marcel Mule (b. 1901), top, began where the saxophone began: in the French Army. In 1928, he formed the first serious saxophone quartet out of the Republican Guard Band, which featured alto, tenor, and baritone, and starred himself on soprano. French teaching abhorred the vibrato, but Mule, taking a cue from classical and operatic vocal soloists, refined the technique for concert playing.

After his army stint was over in 1936, he continued on soprano with his Mule Quartet and on alto in solo appearances. These performances, his many recordings (now out of print), and

a warm personal teaching style won him a certain renown until his retirement in the 1970s. His bright, somewhat metallic tone quality has long been the ideal of the French school of concert artists. If the sax, as some say, is France's national instrument, it is Marcel Mule who made it so.

Marcel Mule premiered Alexander Glazunov's *Quartet* and more than 50 other compositions for classical saxophone.

Cecil Leeson (1902–89), center, was one of the first Americans to earn a degree in saxophone performance and the first in this country to record classical sax music (on Decca 78s in the 1940s). A conservatory teacher since 1926, Leeson was the first saxophonist ever to appear in New York's Town Hall (1937). In 1954 he organized the saxophone program at Northwestern University, today one of the most prestigious anywhere. His interest in the sonata

form led composers to create many such works for alto and the less popular tenor.

A clean, straight-ahead soloist of great tonal purity, Leeson composed music for the saxophone and traced its history in his personal collection of memorabilia and

precious instruments. The Cecil Leeson Collection now resides at the University of South Dakota.

Saxophone compositions premiered by Cecil Leeson include Paul Creston's *Suite* and *Sonata* and more than 40 other titles.

Sigurd Raschèr (b. 1907), bottom, German born and educated, was a clarinetist until he took up the alto in the early 1930s. He was soon using it for harmonic overtones to produce an altissimo register a full octave above the key range. The altissimo, today a required technique for concert saxophonists, was just a part of his greatness. His warmth and richness of tone and his phenomenal speed and flexibility in all registers have been matched by few.

The Nazi era made saxophone music unacceptable in Germany and forced Raschèr overseas, eventually to America. His 1939 Carnegie Hall debut kicked off a concert and teaching

career that lasted until 1981. He made guest appearances with many symphonies, gave the first televised sax recital (over the BBC in the 1940s), and led a noted quartet and large all-sax groups. His playing inspired a so-called German school (mostly American), which offered an alternative to Marcel Mule's style.

Included among works premiered by Sigurd Raschèr are Alexander Glazunov's *Concerto,* Jacques Ibert's *Concertino da Camera,* Ingolf Dahl's *Concerto,* and 70 others.

Mule, Leeson, and Raschèr may never have become household names. The horn may lack a box-office titan like James Galway. And like any post-1800 music, saxophone works are too infrequently heard over classical radio. But to single out the sax is to miss the point. As music history goes, the instrument is a youngster. In its brief existence, it has come very far indeed.

52

The 1920s saxophone boom inspired a wave of music for and about the horn, from forgettable pop ditties to sax arrangements of old favorites.

A 1941 ad in *The Metronome* compares the King Zephyr saxophones to the streamlined trains that inspired their design.

The label design gets the point across perfectly on a 1946 Charlie Ventura recording, far left.

Frank Trumbauer's

Series

For those who couldn't carry a tune, the QRS Piano Company offered the ingenious Playasax. The paper roll did away with fingering — all you had to do was crank and blow.

Sax features prominently on a classic 1940s cocktail shaker, right, which gives an evening at home the carefree air of nightclubbing.

The C. G. Conn Company offered snappy spare-wheel covers to music dealers in 1930.

53

ECLIPSE
METEOR
TAILSPIN
SUNSPOTS
"G" BLUES
KRAZY KAT
TRUMBOLOGY
THREE BLIND MICE
THE BOUNCING BALL
Price 75¢ *each* Net

THE 1940S SAW THE saxophone achieve a near-monopoly on solo jazz. From the '40s to the '60s, most of the music's true innovators played one. A new jazz label, Prestige, even adopted the sax as a logo. The tenor instrument would remain king, proof positive of its unparalleled expressiveness and the mighty influence of Hawkins and Young. But Charlie Parker would bring the alto into its own and create a whole new music: the modern jazz called "bebop," or simply "bop."

The dance music of the swing bands still held the public in its thrall. But modern jazz — sophisticated, challenging, and utterly unsentimental — was making inroads. This new jazz was "head music," while the big bands with their dance-based rhythm and dreamy ballads provided more of a "heart music." Jazz and pop were parting ways once again, with critics now firmly on the side of the new sound.

World War II brought shortages of saxophones as of everything else. The Elkhart factories in Indiana abandoned instrument making and cranked out precision parts for weapons. When the great French Selmer saxes became

Shep Fields's colorful all-reed band of 1940 to 1944 presented a full front line of nine saxophones, above.

Mr. Average Sax Player does his bit for Uncle Sam in a 1942 trade paper advertisement, left.

unavailable, the firm's U.S. plant got around the pad-leather shortage by inventing a Padless Sax. Unfortunately, its cork gaskets leaked badly and the model failed. But the sax stayed alive, even in wartime. Sam Donahue, on tenor sax, led the marvelous swing band of the U.S. Navy. And even in 1942, in occupied Europe, Marcel Mule managed to reactivate Adolphe Sax's courses at the Paris Conservatory. Among his students was Daniel Deffayet (b. 1922), another respected figure in the "French school" of concert artists. Meanwhile in Belgium, François Daneels (b. 1921) was establishing himself as the most prominent soloist from Sax's own country.

At home, a remarkable new band of the early '40s was Shep Fields's all-reed orchestra. Dispensing with the brass altogether, Fields featured four altos, three tenors, one baritone, and one bass saxophonist, doubling in clarinets and flutes to thrilling effect. The band was too experimental to last. But wonderful soloists continued to appear in the swing tradition. Illinois Jacquet (b. 1922) of Lionel Hampton's orchestra took the Ben Webster style to

LESTER YOUNG

HE WAS COOL WHEN COOL WASN'T COOL

In an era of sax kings, Lester Young (1909-59) pretended to no thrones: He was the President of the tenor saxophone.

"Prez" was the total package, from his zoot suits, laid-back demeanor, and hip slang to his relaxed, knowing tenor solos. In an era when Coleman Hawkins's muscular playing was the fashion, Young's playing featured floating phrases and advanced melodic imagination that was less concerned with chord changes than creating new phrases and ideas. With very little vibrato and a fluid, airy tone inspired by Frank Trumbauer's C melody sax, he seemed to play "alto on tenor," even holding the horn at his own odd angle.

His greatest fame came as a member of Count Basie's orchestra and small groups from 1936 to 1940 (on Columbia and Decca CDs, among others), and as a principal in the backup bands of his close friend, Billie Holiday

(Columbia).

A traumatic stateside service in the U.S. Army was nearly Young's undoing as a man and a musician. After World War II, his delicate style began to coarsen and splinter, even as a "cool school" of young tenors such as Stan Getz grew up around him. But Prez was no has-been, as is evident in much of his later work with the likes of Oscar Peterson and Nat King Cole (*Lester Young and the Piano Giants,* Verve). He always kept that special magic — a sound that burned like a cool, blue flame.

a big, broad appeal with his impassioned squeals and shouts, a genre known as Texas tenor after his home state. His signature tune was 1942's *Flying Home,* which anticipated the heated playing of rhythm & blues soloists by ten years. Count Basie had fired Lester Young but found wonderful new tenor talents in Buddy Tate (b. 1915) and Don Byas (1913–72). Of white musicians, the ebullient tenorman Flip Phillips (b. 1915) and Johnny Bothwell, who played a suave, Hodges-type alto, made their mark in 1944 and '45 with two very hip bands, Woody Herman's and Boyd Raeburn's, respectively. Swing music was over only in the sense that something more challenging had been discovered. Quality music was still being made in the genre — for now.

The '40s also saw the first mass-market black music, called "jukebox" or "jump," which married swing rhythm with plain-spoken humor and the simplicity of the blues. The group was small, tight, and always included a saxophone playing in a heated, broad, simple style. The avatar of jump music was Louis Jordan (1908–75), an altoman and singer influenced by Pete Brown, a

CHARLIE PARKER

SHORT FLIGHT OF A GOLDEN BIRD

In his short life (1920–55) Charlie Parker, or "Bird," changed the state of jazz and the voice of the saxophone. In so doing, he became an all-consuming music legend.

First heard in 1940 in Jay McShann's orchestra in his native Kansas City, the largely self-taught Parker was inspired early on by Lester Young's harmonic and melodic innovations. But the style Parker created was a total departure. Never sweet, his tone was edgy, cutting, and at times took on a bluesy roughness. His solos, based on the less-used upper tones of chords, betrayed a lightning-quick mind and a willingness to break the rules of music theory. Today, Parker's style *is* music theory: Young jazz students learn his solos note for note, as painters once studied the Old Masters.

After 1945, Bird's style matured into bebop in partnership with trumpeters Dizzy Gillespie and Miles Davis (*The Complete*

Dial Sessions, Stash; *Parker Memorial*, Savoy). Notable were his many original compositions based on the harmonies of old favorites: *Donna Lee, Koko, Anthropology,* and *Ornithology*. The public enjoyed his sensitive pop interpretations on the 1949 *Charlie Parker with Strings* (Verve).

By the '50s, drugs began to slow Parker, though he still played tremendous music in concerts (*Jazz at Massey Hall*, Prestige). Now, forty years after his passing, virtually every note he ever recorded is available on records. These, along with several biographies, continue to make succeeding generations aware of the Parker phenomenon. Thus the rallying cry of his hard-core devotees: *Bird Lives!*

strong blues-tinged player in the famous music clubs on New York's 52nd Street. Jordan and his Tympani 5 were one of the big success stories of the '40s.

While such players were in the limelight, modern jazz was being born in obscure jam sessions. Dizzy Gillespie on trumpet and Thelonious Monk on piano were crucial to the beginnings of bebop, but the esthetic was Charlie Parker's. Bebop was a saxophonic music: fast, demanding, fleet of phrase, and full of unusual intervals and harmonies. The alto and tenor saxes were simply better suited to it than less facile horns like the clarinet or trombone — which languished as bop brought forth school upon school of fine saxophone innovators.

Parker's impact on saxophonists was as inescapable as Coleman Hawkins's had been ten years before. Alto-men like Sonny Criss and Gigi Gryce owed everything to him. Sonny Stitt (1924–82) was less complicated than Parker but so similar in style that in 1947 he switched to tenor to give himself room to be original. He was that, becoming a favorite of the teenage Sonny Rollins.

Dexter Gordon (1923–90) translated Parker's sound and ideas to the bigger horn. The Gordon tone, thin, pliable, and possessed of tremendous carry and edge, would become the standard in hard-bop and post-bop '50s jazz. His style was the foundation for the music of Sonny Rollins and John Coltrane, and Gordon in turn learned from them as an elder statesman of creative saxophone. He pioneered the

The neon marquee of Bop City in New York, above, heralded a changing of the guard in American music in the late 1940s. Swing was no longer the thing.

Wardell Gray and Dexter Gordon reenact *The Chase*, left. This first of many famous saxophone battles appeared in 1947. Note the period's hipster attire.

fashion for exciting two-tenor battles with Gene Ammons and Wardell Gray, the great example being *The Chase*, with Gray in 1947. Sojourns overseas interrupted Gordon's popularity at home, but a role in the 1986 film *'Round Midnight* crowned his long career with an Oscar nomination.

Another fine bebop tenor saxophone was that of Lucky Thompson (b. 1924), whose career was scarred by mental illness. His approach was inspired by Don Byas, whose luxurious sonority he shared. Wardell Gray (1921–55), a cult favorite among musicians, played with a gorgeous tone that reminded one of Prez even as his improvisations were more modern. The baritone sax also boasted a Parker — Leo Parker (1925–62), no relation to Charlie. He and Cecil Payne (b. 1922) proved that the horn of Harry Carney need not sound Ellingtonian.

These first beboppers were a mostly African-American crowd, with the notable exception of tenorists Georgie Auld (b. 1915) and Charlie Ventura (1916–92). Auld formed his own bop-type band in 1945, whereas Ventura's hybrid swing-to-bop sound

58

THE FOUR BROTHERS
A GREAT SAX SECTION

Jazz's cool school had its beginnings in a radical new big band sax team formed in 1947. Woody Herman's *Four Brothers* band took its name from the hit instrumental written to show off the section of three tenors and one baritone. Their sound was characterized by a Lester Youngish timbre and little vibrato. The tenorists were Stan Getz, Zoot Sims, and Herb Steward, who had briefly played as the Hollywood Sax Quartet (the pioneering classical/jazz crossover group) with *Four Brothers* compos-

er Jimmy Giuffre. Joining them on baritone was Serge Chaloff (1924–57), a somewhat tortured soloist capable of amazing variations in tone and mood.

The Brothers' breezy, highly logical music was very far from the crisp, smoky flavor of Parker's bop. With Stan Getz (1927–91), right, as ringleader, the Herman saxes formed one of the currents in the cool school, a modern jazz incorporating beautifully disciplined ideas and purity of tone. Indeed, Getz's pristine sonori-

ties flowed in a clear, running stream from Lester "Prez" Young, through Frank Trumbauer all the way back to Rudy Wiedoeft. His improvisations were even more laconic and mellow than Young's laid-back jazz.

Getz helped get the bossa-nova style started in this country in the early '60s and he continued into jazz-rock fusion in the

'70s. Among the many he inspired were Al Cohn, Brew Moore, and Allen Eager — all of whom Woody Herman proudly featured at various times. Most famous was Zoot Sims (1925–82), who pulled away from the Getzian pack to play a more robust, Dexter Gordon-inspired saxophone sound, often in a combo he co-led with Al Cohn (1925–88).

Pictured above is the 1948 section with Getz, Cohn, Sam Marowitz (playing Herman's lead alto book), Sims, and Chaloff.

first surfaced in Gene Krupa's band in 1945 and '46. Yet their playing, however good, was largely derivative. The lasting contribution of white sax players to modern jazz was the so-called cool school, whose most important improvisers were saxophonists.

A parallel current in the late '40s was the more theoretical, highly arranged music being created by Miles Davis (1926–91). His 1949 *Birth of the Cool* album (Capitol), informed by his own slyly restrained trumpet style, used the arrangements of Gerry Mulligan (1927-96), a skinny 22-year-old then becoming known for his great baritone saxophone playing. Besides making a name as an arranger and bandleader, Mulligan would come to be *the* player of his instrument. Far different from Harry Carney's huge, rich sound, Mulligan's was woodier in quality, dryly clever in concept. Like his instrument, he was best in a pairing, contextual role, as in his mid-50s quartet with trumpeter Chet Baker and, best of all, his recording sessions with sax greats like Ben Webster and Paul Desmond.

Another Miles Davis sideman was Lee Konitz (b. 1927), not so much a cool-schooler as a total original. Coming from a classical clarinet background, Konitz strove for utter purity of tone and execution, playing a serene, glassy alto with barely a hint of vibrato. In 1949 he joined the group of Lennie Tristano, who sought to combine bop with the rigor of academic music theory. With Warne Marsh (1927–87), his counterpart on tenor, Konitz combined an austere beauty with the inescapable influence of Parker. Still blowing, he has also become a prominent jazz educator.

Cool music, along with bebop and its stylistic heirs, remained a continuing trend into the 1950s — a decade especially rich in sound as new saxophone music came to co-exist with the old.

Miles Davis cools it with Lee Konitz and Gerry Mulligan (left to right) in their groundbreaking 1949 band, below.

The saxophone seems made for the movies. It has inspired whole feature films, from Martin Scorsese's nostalgic "New York, New York" (1977), where Georgie

"'Round Midnight," real-life legend Dexter Gordon brought believability to the role of a fictitious jazz veteran. The definitive saxophone movie, some say, has yet to be

SAX IN THE MOVIES

60

Auld dubbed the playing for Robert De Niro's sharpie tenorman (this page), to the factually-based "Bird" (1988), Clint Eastwood's account of the life of Charlie Parker. In the 1986 film

made. But famous sax scenes figure in many films. Those pictured opposite illustrate the many facets of the instrument — silly, seductive, warm, lonesome, and always human.

Opposite, clockwise from top left:

Heaven Can Wait, 1978
Warren Beatty gives out a shaky serenade for Julie Christie.

Son of Flubber, 1962
Former big band sideman Fred MacMurray plays it for laughs. Not until New York, New York did a big-time movie have a sax player as hero.

'Round Midnight, 1986
Dexter Gordon is the archetypal American jazzman in Europe. The role won him an Oscar nomination and a new generation of fans.

Moscow on the Hudson, 1984
Robin Williams is a Russian circus musician who defects.

Hurry Sundown, 1969
Jane Fonda and Michael Caine say it with music.

SAXOPHONE

THE MODERN SAXOPHONE

CHARLIE PARKER, THE FIRST MODERN SAXOPHONIST, left a rich legacy for the next generation's artists, significantly enhancing the instrument's tradition. By the '60s, the decade of John Coltrane, the saxophone would become music's starship, traveling with its players into unimagined realms of pure sound. ▣ In the face of the free-jazz revolution, old ways of playing appeared to be over. But that view no longer holds. With a century and a half of history to draw on, we revel in the saxophone's rich diversity of tones and moods. ▣ And we became more sax-conscious than ever when jammin' Bill Clinton, armchair saxman extraordinaire, became leader of the Free World.

The Presidential jam, opposite, included tenor legend Illinois Jacquet (left) and rising young jazzman Joshua Redman (right), representing half a century of saxophone history. In his first year in office, Clinton played sax on national TV, in Boris Yeltsin's Kremlin, and on his own CD release. Music stores featured Presidential Series mouthpieces and a special edition of red, white, and blue enameled L.A. Sax tenors.

65

The magnificent 1950s Count Basie reed section, previous pages, immortalized *April in Paris* and many other late-day big band classics.

Julian "Cannonball" Adderley, above, altoman supreme, helped define the esthetic of Hard Bop in the '50s.

Paul Desmond and his leader, Dave Brubeck, left, became famous for their finely crafted, classically inspired sax-piano duets. Desmond's wit and humor gave the Brubeck group much of its character.

THE LATEST CURRENT IN SAXOPHONE music as the '50s got underway was California's take on the cool school, West Coast jazz. Saxophone voices were crucial to the short-lived Gerry Mulligan-Chet Baker Quartet, as well as to the success of the Dave Brubeck Quartet with Paul Desmond (1924–77) on alto. In an era of would-be Charlie Parkers, Desmond felt drawn to Lee Konitz's intellectually driven sax language. His tonal ideal, as he put it, was "to sound like a dry martini," and his improvising was clever and lyrical. His recording of *Take Five* with Brubeck was a tremendous hit in 1961 but left him stereotyped by the public.

West Coast jazz showed its more commercial side in big band recordings by top Los Angeles studio musicians such as trumpeter "Shorty" Rogers, whose key soloists were Art Pepper's alto, Bud Shank's alto and flute, and Bob Cooper's tenor. All were products of the very popular Stan Kenton band of the '40s. Art Pepper (1925–82) was the most influential, with his smoothed-out, understated variation on the Parker style. In the

'60s, he began to be influenced by John Coltrane's playing. Sadly, like many others, he fell prey to drug abuse, and even served a prison term before reappearing in the '70s.

The Hollywood Saxophone Quartet, which included Stan Getz among its members, bridged the often alienated worlds of jazz and classical music, premiering original works in both idioms and releasing major-label recordings. Meanwhile in academia, composers' interest in saxophone sounds continued to grow, and American universities were starting to add the instrument to their music curricula. By 1953, Larry Teal, a former radio studio musician, was head of the new sax curriculum at the University of Michigan. Cecil Leeson accepted the job of saxophone professor at Northwestern University the next year. The less tradition-bound midwestern schools started the trend, and their first virtuosi are today at the forefront of the American classical saxophone. In the '50s, new concert soloists of a high order also emerged in England and Canada, as well as a second generation in France.

It was still too early for much original repertory to be played. What did exist tended to focus on the alto as the only acceptable solo voice, a phenomenon that persists because of the emphasis on alto playing in the college curriculum. Other voices found expression in the increasingly widespread saxophone quartet clinics and recitals.

While classical saxophone playing, both in repertoire and technique, was growing, pop saxophone was losing its way. Mood music, popular as at-home recorded entertainment, was an imitative re-creation of pre-war pop colors and tempos that were reminiscent of an earlier era's subdued accompaniments to romantic singers. It used saxes as a bland cushion of soft harmony, or as a solo-voice cliché connoting the "sultry sax." In short, mood music affected the mannerisms of jazz but none of its creativity.

The mood music phenomenon did produce one excellent soloist in Freddy Gardner (1912–50), the English altoist who had played excellent jazz in Ray Noble's '30s band. Gardner's powerful and limpid tone was featured uniformly in ballads, his smooth

Crossover sax music of the '50s included the easy-listening sounds of the Four Freshmen, with sax section colors added, right.

King Curtis, below, and Earl Bostic, below right, were two lasting contributors to rhythm & blues and early rock.

delivery augmented by a new device, audio reverb. Saxophone concept albums also enjoyed '50s success. Bobby Dukoff, a big band veteran, had a whole series, including *Sax in Silk* and *Sax in Satin*. Hollywood arrangers experimented with sax ensemble sessions, the biggest being Pete Rugolo's *10 Saxophones and 2 Basses* (Mercury).

African-Americans — and, increasingly, young whites as well — began to turn to the rougher, more exciting sound of rhythm & blues, the music

that paved the way for rock & roll. Techniques of this genre such as double fingering, honking (the rhythmic repetition of one low note), and unfettered exhibitionism were the hallmarks of "Big Jay" McNeely, who began wowing California audiences in 1951 with choreographed antics like playing on top of tables while lying on his back. Red Prysock, Willis "Gator Tail" Jackson, and many more followed in Big Jay's vein. King Curtis was a capable jazzman who found Top 40 fame in the rock & roll era playing backup for The Coasters with teen hits such as *Yakety Yak* and *Charlie Brown* (Atlantic Records). Meanwhile, jump music was perpetuated by two alto players. Earl Bostic, whose late-'40s band had included John Coltrane, had a hit record in 1954 with his rendering of Franz Liszt's *Liebestraum*. Tab Smith, a superb jazzman with Count Basie in the '40s, cut singles that featured ballads and the inevitable 12-bar blues.

In 1955, Charlie Parker was dead at the age of 35. The saxophone scene he left behind was a grand mosaic, richer and more varied in tonality. Besides the continuing experimentation in modern jazz, the '50s saw the last great flourishing of swing soloists. The financial drawbacks of big band music, coupled with the highly political jazz climate of the '60s, would spell the end of the dear old school of Hawkins, Webster, and Young.

At the top of this last graduating class was Paul Gonsalves (1920–74), Duke Ellington's tenor soloist from 1950 on. A consistently exciting and intelligent player, Gonsalves may have

The always exciting Johnny Griffin showed the style that made him a tenorman of unparalleled technique, above.

Pepper Adams, left, redefined the sound of the baritone in the '50s. But the difficult instrument still intimidated other players. Benny Golson and Art Farmer, opposite, lead their hard-bop group, the Jazztet, in 1961.

been Ben Webster's greatest pupil, adding tonal elegance to the powerful, shouting style until it positively glowed. Renowned for a marathon 27-chorus solo on the album *Ellington at Newport* (Columbia), Gonsalves had a singular style as well as enviable endurance.

Count Basie continued presenting us with fine sax playing. Marshall Royal (1912–95), one of the truly great lead altos, headed up a sterling section notable for a parade of tenor soloists. Eddie "Lockjaw" Davis (1930–86), a hard-bitten Illinois Jacquet follower, shared the early '50s section with Paul Quinichette (1916–83), who was such an eloquent student of Lester Young that he was nicknamed Vice-Prez to Young's Prez. Frank Foster (b. 1928), a capable man in the early-bop idiom, and Frank Wess (b. 1922), an easy stylist also renowned for his flute playing, were known simply as "the Franks" to most Basie followers. With the Count gone, Foster today is the leader of the Basie "ghost" band.

In Charlie Parker's absence, small-combo music was blessed with a new generation of players on the alto sax. Julian "Cannonball" Adderley

(1928–75) may have been the best. With his trumpeter brother Nat, Julian led a popular quintet with a funkier, less intellectually rarefied approach to bebop. Hard bop, or post-bop, brought the heart back to what had mellowed into head music. Adderley's playing, building on the soulful, blues side of the Parker tradition, informed players like Phil Woods (b. 1930). Woods's varied career includes even a Top 40 hit: the sax solo in Billy Joel's *Just the Way You Are.* The plaintive crying quality of Jackie McLean (b. 1932) was prominent in Charles Mingus's group. McLean has since become a prominent music educator.

A hard-hitting, post-bop group, Art Blakey's Jazz Messengers supplied excellent tenor soloists starting in 1955 with Johnny Griffin (b. 1928). The 5-foot 3-inch "little giant" possesses a love for up tempos and an inexhaustible, punchy energy. Griffin's adopted country of France has given him a huge following. Also out of the Blakey band came the rounder-toned Hank Mobley (1930–86) and Benny Golson (b. 1929). Golson's great playing is often overlooked in favor of his

Paul Gonsalves, the last of a line descending from Hawkins and Webster, was with Duke Ellington until 1974.

equally formidable composing and arranging talents.

The baritone saxophone had a new adherent in Pepper Adams (1930–86). Unmindful of the instrument's reputation as a clumsy juggernaut, he played like a tenorman, with great speed and a dry, crispy attack. In the mid-50s, too, the soprano sax made its debut in modern music with the experiments of Lucky

Thompson and, most notably, Steve Lacy (b. 1934), a one-time Sidney Bechet fan whose 1957 album *Soprano Sax* explored the quirky, introspective possibilities of the straight horn.

Soprano Sax was one of a raft of jazz-sax concept albums that appeared in the late '50s. The most popular trend was the two-tenor battle, which featured spirited blowing competitions. Gene Ammons and Sonny Stitt were a legendary pairing, as were Johnny Griffin and Eddie "Lockjaw" Davis. Phil Woods and Gene Quill were a frequent alto pairing, and of course Gerry Mulligan partnered with just about every sax giant on records.

The sax sound of the '60s was presaged by an LP called *Tenor Madness,* which was released in 1956. This Prestige album brought together Sonny Rollins and John Coltrane, two young men who would usher in the next era of the saxophone. Rollins, age 25, would pioneer a new way to play the instrument, whereas John Coltrane, almost 30, was searching for new approaches to music itself. At decade's end, music's cutting edge was poised at the tip of a saxophone reed once again.

70

SONNY ROLLINS
SAXOPHONE COLOSSUS

Out of the rich ferment of bebop and post-bop came a titan who redefined the sound of the tenor sax in jazz. Theodore "Sonny" Rollins (b. 1930) did for the tenor what Charlie Parker had done for the alto sax.

Rollins's early idols were bop tenors Sonny Stitt and Dexter Gordon. But after hearing the stark dissonances and silences of the early '50s Thelonious Monk combo, Sonny applied the new ideas to his sax. Where the boppers played lots of notes, he played fewer. Where they spun long linear runs, Rollins built upon motifs: basic, meaty phrases on which he elaborated with his thick, rich, highly changeable tone and popping attack. John Coltrane would draw much inspiration from the younger Rollins.

The 1954 Miles Davis set *Bags' Groove* (Prestige) showcased Rollins's original tunes. But his 1956 to 1957 albums —

Saxophone Colossus, Way Out West, and *Tenor Madness* with John Coltrane and others (all Prestige) — made him the sax player to watch. Then, in 1959, he dropped out of sight for two years to study composition. By his return,

Coltrane and the "new thing" had captured the attention — and the ears — of the intelligentsia. Sonny's more tonal jazz was largely neglected until the 1970s, when he reappeared on the scene with an electrified jazz-fusion group.

Rollins today is an elder statesman of the saxophone. A 1986 film documentary chronicled his career, and although his concert appearances aren't as frequent as one might wish, he is surely the most influential tenorman alive.

AS SOCIAL AND POLITICAL tensions grew in the '60s, African-American musicians continued affirming their own cultural identity, one apart from white show biz and the songs of Tin Pan Alley. This desire was expressed in a new music that shunned European music's formal structure and intellectualism in favor of the freedom of pure sound and emotion. And in this pre-electronic era, the instrument of choice, of necessity really, was the saxophone.

Altoist Ornette Coleman (b. 1930) defined the new esthetic and named it with his Atlantic album *Free Jazz*. A self-taught former rhythm & blues tenorman, Coleman and his quartet debuted their collective improvisational style in New York in 1958 with a non-chordal, non-time music that many listeners understood only as noise. Ornette's alto could be particularly harrowing with its intense, emotional caterwauling. But those who listened more closely could hear Coleman's incredible range of expression and the tidal flow of ideas coursing among the group's members.

It wasn't just noise, affirmed his fans: It was "harmolodics," a music

Polo Ralph Lauren's classy tie, left, is complemented by a handsome sax clasp by Eclipse of New Zealand.

Souvenirs of Memphis and New Orleans, use the saxophone to remind us of those cities' jazz heritages.

No living president can appear on a stamp, but this 1992 Bill Clinton campaign button, right, was a great idea — as was the nifty 18" statuette, top.

Smooth Jazz
CD 101.9 ™

With an Adult-Contemporary mix featuring such artists as David Sanborn, Kenny G, and Grover Washington, New York's WQCD-FM is one station where you can hear sax music almost any time you tune in, above right.

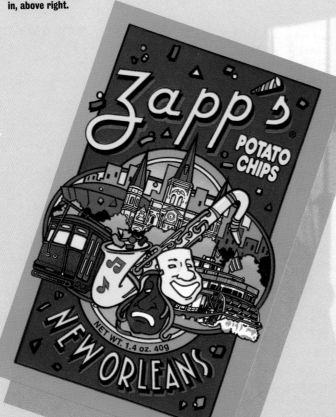

where the solo melodic tail wags the harmonic dog. Over the years, Coleman has carried his philosophy over to the trumpet and violin, to his electronic group Primetime, and into collaboration with jazz-fusion guitarist Pat Metheny.

One of Coleman's early admirers was Eric Dolphy (1928–64), whose vaulting, squealing alto solos were more grounded in bebop and more accessible. He infused jazz with the deep purple liquidity of the bass clarinet, and he was one of many doublers who moved to the flute. His work with Charles Mingus's band is exceptionally fine, as is his own album *Out To Lunch!* (Blue Note).

By 1965 many players were absorbing the lessons of Coltrane, Coleman, and Dolphy. The Association for the Advancement of Creative Music featured altoist Anthony Braxton (b. 1945), a composer-educator who idolized Lee Konitz. Braxton and fellow alto Roscoe Mitchell assembled the most impressive arsenal of doubles since the sax-daffy '20s. Mitchell revived interest in the bass sax, while Braxton's forest of woodwinds has

included the contrabass and sopranino.

In his last years, John Coltrane assembled numerous tenor acolytes. Among them was Archie Shepp (b. 1937), who mixed his agonizingly raw music with poetry and polemics. He has since branched out to reinterpret more traditional idioms. Coltrane's protegé, Pharaoh Sanders (b. 1940), is similarly intense, though his work does not reflect the full scope and fire of Coltrane's music. Albert Ayler (1936–70), a boisterous player, loved gospel, rhythm & blues, and New Orleans brass bands, and his compositions freely mixed these eclectic sounds.

Other free-jazzers include alto-men Marion Brown, John Tchicai, and Sonny Simmons, as well as tenormen Dewey Redman and Sam Rivers. Rahsaan Roland Kirk (1936–77), however, was in his own category. Often playing three saxes at once, he added to the tenor two modified '20s horns: the Manzello, a King Saxello soprano, and a Buescher straight alto he called the Stritch. The outrageous Kirk might play New Orleans clarinet one minute and lip-buzz a reedless sax the

The uncompromising abstractionism of Ornette Coleman, above, was less understandable to traditional musicians than the playing of Eric Dolphy, right, on alto sax, flute, and bass clarinet. Together with John Coltrane, Coleman and Dolphy led the saxophone avant-garde.

74

JOHN COLTRANE

THE LAST MESSIAH?

To John Coltrane (1926-67), music was a spiritual quest very near life's essence. Among jazz's fathers, in a line from Armstrong through Parker, "Trane" is regarded as the latest. A new discovery at 30, by 40 the soft-spoken tenorman and composer was gone.

He first achieved renown with the 1955 to 1959 Miles Davis group (*Kind of Blue*, Columbia) after years in rhythm & blues. He and Sonny Rollins were close kin at the beginning, Trane having a thinner tone and more austere, fragmentary phrasing. Never content, he practiced so hard he often fell asleep with the horn around his neck.

That inner drive helped him overcome substance-abuse problems and find new ways of understanding music. 1959's *Giant Steps* (Atlantic) was his last excursion into chord harmony. His famous quartet (debuting in 1960 on *My Favorite Things*, Atlantic) helped establish modal jazz, where scales replaced chords as a base for improvisation.

Coltrane also took up the soprano sax after hearing Steve Lacy. Traditionalists sneered at his quirky, convoluted playing, but Trane was the prime reason for the revival of the little horn.

After 1964, Coltrane became a leader in the sax-based free jazz. He pioneered multiphonics (blowing dual frequencies) and the exploration of South Asian music (*A Love Supreme*, Impulse!). His "sheets of sound" — continuous skeins of unarticulated notes — left early fans confused. He spent his last years completely immersed in the tonal possibilities of the saxophone, which he explored to the limit.

Coltrane was and is a role model for African-Americans who wanted to reclaim jazz from the white culture. Today he is revered and respected, if not always understood.

next. Blind from birth, he always said his music came to him in his dreams.

But the freedom sound of African-American jazzists was not the whole story of the '60s saxophone. Few white players espoused the largely black style, Steve Lacy being one exception. The turmoil of the times often played out along racial and political lines, even more so than today.

The concert saxophone world seemed very removed from all this. Its second generation included three of today's most respected teacher-virtuosi: Eugene Rousseau (b. 1932) of Indiana University, Frederick Hemke (b. 1935) of Northwestern University, and Jean-Marie Londeix (b. 1931), late of the Bordeaux Conservatory. All were students of Marcel Mule, the pioneer who helped the brilliant-toned French school gain dominance in academic music.

The New York Saxophone Quartet, begun in 1960, continued the Hollywood Quartet tradition of mixing jazz and academic music. And the London Saxophone Quartet, founded in 1968 by Paul Harvey, gave concert playing its first real exposure in Great

Rahsaan Roland Kirk, far left, the one-man musical movement, played a televised concert in Europe in 1975.

Steve Lacy, center, was one of comparatively few white players to be in on free jazz during the early years. Many followed in the '70s and after.

The tenor and soprano of Wayne Shorter, near left, have been heard most often in his own original compositions.

76

Britain. Yet there was no real classical saxophone community and no serious attempt to build the horn's reputation. The first World Saxophone Congress in Chicago in 1969 marked the beginning of the end for that cloistered era.

This was not the ideal decade to be starting out as a mainstream jazz player. There was already an overabundance of good sax musicians from the '50s, many of whom were still mostly ignored. One who won some fame was Yusef Lateef (b. 1921), a swing-generation tenorman who is also jazz's only notable oboist. Joe Henderson (b. 1937), a one-time Lateef associate, fell into obscurity despite a series of '60s Blue Note albums revealing a highly melodic, thoughtful tenor. Yet, except for a passing tonal resemblance to Sonny Rollins, he fit into no recognizable school; in an era of categories, Henderson just did not belong. A 1993 Grammy Award for his CD *Lush Life* (Verve) finally brought this great tenor saxophonist to the attention of today's listening public.

The intelligent tenor and sopra-no work of Wayne Shorter (b. 1933) won few fans until he joined Miles Davis in 1964, where he became known for his spare, elegant compositions. From 1970 to 1985, Shorter co-led Weather Report, perhaps the best of the '70s fusion bands, which employed him less as a solo voice than as a texture in the ensemble. Though many considered fusion, a hybrid of rock and jazz, beneath Shorter, he has had a significant impact on today's mainstream players.

But in the '60s, mainstream pop,

David Sanborn, opposite, may be the biggest pure pop sax sensation since Rudy Wiedoeft. Since the '70s, he has certainly been the most recognizable name to the public.

But in the '60s, mainstream pop, submerged in the youth culture of guitar rock, all but ignored the sax. The Grateful Dead were an occasional exception. Another was Nashville, where Boots Randolph put out easy-listening LPs with a country twang. His big hit, *Yakety Sax,* proved that in any era, there's room for at least one snappy sax novelty.

African-American pop, including rhythm & blues and the new soul music, was enriched by crossover sax players who could also blow bluesy jazz. The tenor/organ genre was enlivened by Stanley Turrentine (b. 1934), often accompanied by organist-wife Shirley Scott. Hank Crawford (b. 1934), a cooking alto player with an arresting ballad style, toured with Ike and Tina Turner and Ray Charles and was a prime influence on David Sanborn. King Curtis was a continuing presence, while Junior Walker (1942–95) led the Motown-styled All Stars. Then there was Eddie Harris (b. 1934), known for his use of the Selmer Varitone. This huge amplified box was the first attempt to apply electronic technology to an instrument that never really needed it.

SAXOPHONE FANS OFTEN speak of the '70s as the low point in the industry's history. Jazz began to drift in the '60s, losing itself to electronic, rock, and folk influences. But while saxes also lost ground to amplified flutists like Herbie Mann, they gained a higher profile in pop music, as bands like Chicago adopted horn sections. And saxes were still at the heart of jazz, even as that much-abused word came to stand for a bewildering diversity of sounds.

The saxophone '70s seemed to crystallize in altoist David Sanborn (b. 1945) and tenorman Michael Brecker (b. 1949). Sanborn is the pop-rock player of *Saturday Night Live* fame and other TV gigs. He lays out melodies with direct simplicity and a sizzling, penetrating tone. Mike Brecker, more a jazzman, defined a new kind of sax musicianship, polishing the lessons of John Coltrane with a session-man's flawless discipline. Moving with equal ease in jazz and commercial music, he has been a model for countless young players trying to tackle a fiercely demanding music industry.

While Wayne Shorter was the big name in fusion music, this genre also gave us Dave Liebman (b. 1946), a tenor and soprano player who now concentrates on the smaller horn. John Klemmer (b. 1946) made new age music with solo tenor and the electronic Echoplex device, while Tom Scott (b. 1948) dabbled with the Lyricon, the first true electronic wind instrument. More of a pop artist, Grover

saxmen who make a place for the horn in the Latin music of their homelands. British baritonist John Surman (b. 1944) incorporates free-jazz and folk-music elements in his work. Furthest from jazz is Norwegian tenorman Jan Garbarek (b. 1947), whose minimalist music is evocative of the stark poetry and melodies of Norse folk songs.

The '70s also gave birth to Supersax, a quintet known for transcriptions of Charlie Parker solos.

Tenorman Scott Hamilton (b. 1954) draws on a wealth of idioms from the work of Hawkins to Zoot Sims. His superb musicianship has won him exceptional critical acclaim. A star on the Concord label, he has

A vital part of Bruce Springsteen's Top 40 sound was his tenor soloist, Clarence Clemons, far left.

Michael Brecker, center, combines a post-60s jazz esthetic with the uncompromising perfectionism of the studio musician.

The only Argentinian sax player to win world renown, Gato Barbieri, near left, is one of many who helped open the field for non-Americans in the '70s.

Washington, Jr., has been a compelling, soul-tinged instrumentalist on soprano, alto, and tenor.

The move to world music — music reflecting international as opposed to American influences — brought to prominence Argentina's Gato Barbieri (b. 1934) and Cuba's Paquito d'Rivera (b. 1948), composer-

A '70s boom in revivalist players stirred interest in past styles. In *Soprano Summit*, the soprano saxes of Bob Wilber and Kenny Davern elaborated on the lessons of Sidney Bechet with great originality. Altoist Richie Cole (b. 1948) was promoted as the harbinger of a hard-bop revival that ultimately failed to materialize.

worked with Benny Goodman and Rosemary Clooney, as well as his own groups. In 1974, Joe Temperley (b. 1929) assumed Harry Carney's baritone spot in the Duke Ellington Orchestra. And the bass sax found a new voice in Vince Giordano (b. 1952), a soloist with his own '20s- and '30s-style big band.

Sax education — jazz and classical — took a step forward at home and abroad with the founding of the North American Saxophone Alliance and the Association de Saxophonistes de France. Meanwhile, soloists like John Sampen (b. 1949) gave the saxophone a role in the wide-open field of electronic concert music. With synthesizers still

SINCE 1980, THE SHEER NUMBER and variety of saxophone players have reached an all-time peak. Jazz, particularly that of Sonny Rollins and John Coltrane, remains the dominant sound, probably for all time. Yet more kinds of music for the saxophone thrive than ever. Artists blend styles once thought irreconcilable. Some find the

Yamaha WX11 are versatile wrinkles but they are not a substitute for the real thing. *Sax* is one setting that seldom appears on an emulator keyboard.

An exemplar of the eclecticism that is jazz sax today is the World Saxophone Quartet, begun in 1977, whose repertoire ranges from free jazz to African music to Ellingtonian

An unabashed swing stylist is Scott Hamilton, left, today's premier exponent of pre-bop tenor playing.

Harbingers of a new trend to sax ensembles were the World Saxophone Quartet, right, with leader David Murray on tenor, in 1982.

rare, saxophonists often performed live over an accompaniment recorded on reel-to-reel tape.

And the end of an era came when the veteran Sigurd Raschèr laid down his horn in 1981, even as Dave Bilger (b. 1945) and others of the Raschèr school carried on in the master's velvety-toned, rhapsodic style.

result a meaningless mush, others see it as a creative magic carpet ride. If the brainchild of Adolphe Sax is often taken for granted, that only proves how fundamental it has become to music.

The coming of age of synthesizers and MIDI computers has hurt the popularity of saxophone hardly at all. Electronic wind instruments like the

harmonies. Its tenorman and bass clarinetist, David Murray (b. 1955) has earned great acclaim. Where other saxophone players explore different styles from piece to piece, Murray synthesizes them from moment to moment. Alto-sopranoist Julius Hemphill (1938-95), who left the group in 1990, did much to define with Murray its polyglot esthetic, which features woodwind doubles.

The World Saxophone Quartet set the stage for a revival in sax ensembles. The mainstream 29th Street Saxophone Quartet introduced Bobby Watson, a showmanly, extroverted alto player now leading his own combo, Horizon. The sax-tet wave also gave us the avant-garde quartet Rova, the seven-sax

Odean Pope Chorus, and the Nuclear Whales Saxophone Orchestra, six richly entertaining San Franciscans who blend jazz, light classics, and comedy. Largest of the groups is Urban Sax, whose performance-art happenings of up to thirty *saxtronauts* are a favorite with French audiences.

After the profusion of dime-store Coltranes of the '70s, Sonny Rollins's more traditionally based playing has won new appreciation in the past decade and a half. Definitely in Sonny's tradition is Branford Marsalis (b. 1960), whose tenor and soprano first surfaced in Art Blakey's Jazz Messengers alongside his trumpeter brother, Wynton Marsalis. Like Wynton, Branford has become a huge celebrity. He has led the *Tonight Show* band, appeared with Sting and his own groups, and has educated cable-TV viewers about the sax tradition in two specials, *Reed Royalty* and *Tenor Titans*.

The tenor sax's range, power, and unparalleled expressiveness ensure its status as the number-one instrument for creative jazz. Lionized as its next great has been Joshua Redman (b. 1969), a discovery of the early '90s and the son of tenorman Dewey Redman. This imaginative young player is a Harvard graduate who barely touched the horn during his college years, yet he quickly convinces audiences of his ability to help carry the tenor tradition into a new century.

A concise summary of the wide-ranging and eclectic jazz saxophone scene of the past decade is difficult if not impossible. Our present-day artists must be heard to be truly appreciated. And, for every player mentioned, a dozen more immediately come to mind. How to navigate this sea of creativity? The only answer is to jump in, open your ears, and go where the music takes you.

One venue is concert music, in which saxophones have been steadily

Concert artist and clinician Dave Bilger, left, demonstrates the 1927 Buescher straight alto for his students.

The San Francisco Saxophone Quartet, center, prove the instrument's adaptability by playing music written before the sax even existed.

Jazz ignored Joe Henderson, near left, for too long. Now he's known as a true original in a field where imitation is the rule.

Can true jazz sax make it in the public market? Personable Branford Marsalis, opposite, seems to have done just that in the '90s.

trengthening their presence. Dave Bilger's 17-piece Saxophone Sinfonia has appeared at New York's Lincoln Center, a first for a large sax choir, while groups in France and Austria also work in the large format. The CD era means that academic and recital music is better documented than ever before. Englishman John Harle (b. 1956) is easily the most prolific recorder, while small-label CDs offer a staggering array of soloists and ensembles, including the respected Chicago, Berlin, and San Francisco quartets. The last transcribed baroque favorites attract the traditional listener, while their free public performances take the music to the streets. In France, Claude Delangle (b. 1957) is the most prominent soloist today in the tradition of Marcel Mule. The country of Holland, which took Ben Webster and Don Byas to its heart, boasts a lively saxophone scene, as do Germany, Italy, Austria, and, of course, Belgium.

A surge of popularity came with America's election in 1992 of a saxophone-playing president. (Bill Clinton was not the first world leader to

blow the horn; the King of Thailand played one for years.) Given that a busy officeholder can't take time to practice, Clinton's campaign appearances with tenor in hand did much to accent his youthful appeal. His inaugural jam, his visit to the Selmer factory, and his impromptu recital at the Kremlin made saxomaniacs feel that their instrument had arrived in very high places indeed. The President didn't start the '90s boom that put sax sounds at the top of the pop charts. But he certainly hasn't harmed the ubiquitous Kenny G, the soprano-playing pied piper who has spread awareness of the horn to many, especially the young.

The saxophone's possibilities range far beyond what Adolphe Sax could have imagined puttering in his workshop. The ugly duckling with the beautiful call has taken over the world. Growing, multiplying, ever changing, it has become as big and endlessly rich as music itself — yet is still as familiar as one's own voice. Indeed, few sounds have come to mean so much to so many as the sound of a saxophone.

SAX OBJECTS

SAXOPHONES ARE EVERYWHERE WE LISTEN. It is no surprise, then, to find them everywhere we look. ▣ The instrument is a visual symbol of rich significance. Pop culture from television to advertising uses it as a quick association to all things "jazzy." The simple sight of  a sax, like its sound, can touch us deeply. ▣ Its sinuous curves evoke the elegance of the swan or the seductiveness of the serpent. Its intricacy of keys and rods hints at the complexity of the music it can make. Its voice can be as penetrating as the shine of its brass when new, or as mellow as its well-used patina when old. ▣ This chapter is a montage of images to remind us of the saxophone's rich life in our culture.

85

Soft Saxophone:
Claes Oldenburg.
Sculptor Claes
Oldenburg burst
upon the '60s Pop
Art scene with
his singular depic-
tions of common
household objects.
This 1992 litho-
graph is his treat-
ment of a most
familiar — and
popular — musical
entity.

Umber Blues:
Sonny in the Middle,
Larry Rivers.
Known as both a
jazz bassist and a
painter, Larry
Rivers has been
one of relatively
few artists to
explore the horn's
possibilities, as in
this 1987
multiplane relief.

87

Quiet Calvin Coolidge was hardly the whoopee type. So this 1925 *Life* magazine cartoon by C. H. Sykes is doubly comical for its depiction of our 30th president tooting the horn for capitalism. The saxophone's power as an image made this one of the great political cartoons of all time.

"YES, SIR, HE'S MY BABY!"

Bill Clinton took the GOP elephant by the snout in 1992, when Ben Sargent's cartoon, opposite center, appeared in the *Austin American-Statesman.*

Lisa Simpson, right, has little competition as the best baritone sax player on television.

88

George Herriman's *Krazy Kat* comic of April 12, 1920, shows Krazy and Ignatz Mouse finding new uses for the "sexophone."

Harry Haenigsen chronicled the progress of the saxophone in a classic cartoon for the *New York World* in 1927. And he did make a valid point, especially in the celestial realm. A harp sounds nice, but it's hard to play.

89

By the time this 1932 Hallmark card appeared, the '20s sax fad was good and over, but the horn still added cheer to birthday wishes. Note the delicate rose "engraving" on the bell.

A chocolate saxophone by Mardi Gras Candies proclaims New Orleans's status as birthplace of jazz. Even though the instrument was never a part of authentic Dixieland music, there's no shaking the association in the public mind.

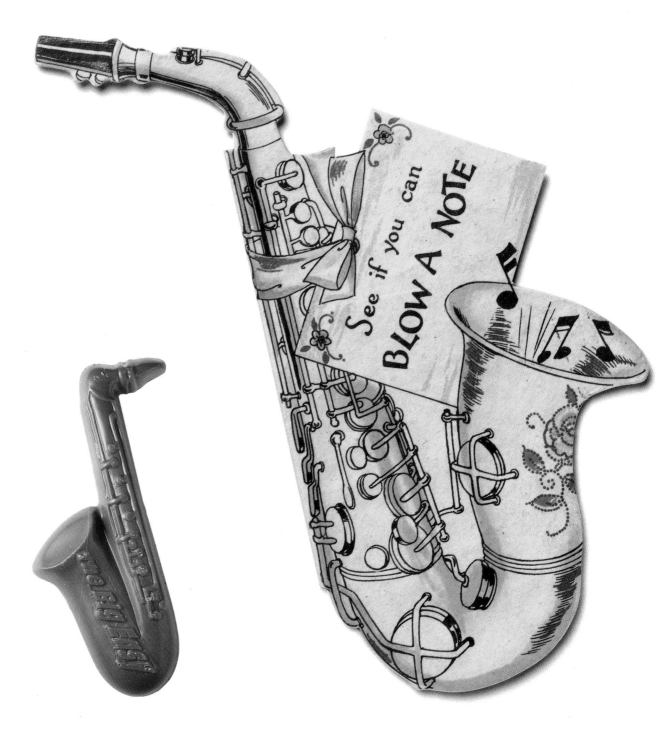

See if you can BLOW A NOTE

This wonderful stamp from The Netherlands was part of a 1992 series celebrating children and musical instruments.

In 1994 —— a hundred years after the passing of Sax —— his native town of Dinant was the scene of an extravaganza. In honor of this long-neglected native son, Albert, King of festival, and an international classical solo competition helped remind the world of Sax's immense contribution to music. A public square was named for him. But perhaps most

THE YEAR OF SAX

the Belgians, proclaimed the International Year of Adolphe Sax. For months the placid rock-walled city on the River Meuse played host to an onslaught of music, musicians —— and saxophones. A day of bands, a jazz

1994 ANNEE
ADOLPHE SAX
DINANT BELGIQUE

moving was the last night of festivities. On the anniversary of Adolphe Sax's birth, the center of town resounded with the music of a thousand saxophones, singing in tribute to the genius who created them.

RECOMMENDED READING

THE FOLLOWING LIST of books in English on saxophonists and the saxophone is by no means comprehensive. But it will give some feel for the instrument's tradition and leading artists.

Berger, Edward, and Monroe Berger. *Benny Carter: A Life In American Music.* Lanham, MD: Scarecrow Press, 1982.

Chilton, John. *Song of the Hawk: The Life and Recordings of Coleman Hawkins.* Ann Arbor: University of Michigan Press, 1990.

Chilton, John. *Sidney Bechet: The Wizard of Jazz.* New York: Oxford University Press, 1987.

Cole, Bill. *John Coltrane.* New York: Da Capo Press, 1993.

Gee, Harry R. *Saxophone Soloists and Their Music, 1844–1985.* Bloomington: Indiana University Press, 1986.

Giddins, Gary. *Celebrating Bird: The Triumph of Charlie Parker.* New York: Quill/Beech Tree Books, 1987.

Ray Nelson's Bear Mountain Orchestra, together for 29 years, typified the Saturday night gig bands that employed thousands of semi-professional sax players.

Horwood, Wally. *Adolphe Sax: 1814–1894.* Baldock, Herts., England: Egon Publishers, 1987.

Klinkowitz, Jerome. *Listen: Gerry Mulligan.* New York: Schirmer Books, 1991.

Kool, Jaap. *Das Saxophon (The Saxophone),* translated by Lawrence Gwozdz. Baldock, Herts., England: Egon Publishers, 1987.

Litweiler, John. *Ornette Coleman: A Harmolodic Life.* New York: William Morrow, 1992.

Londeix, Jean-Marie. *150 Years of Music for the Saxophone.* Cherry Hill, NJ: Roncorp Publications, 1994.

Porter, Lewis, ed. *A Lester Young Reader.* Washington: Smithsonian Institution Press, 1991.

Rousseau, Eugene. *Marcel Mule: His Life and the Saxophone.* St. Louis: MMB Music Publishers, 1993.

Jazz reference books are invaluable in learning about saxophone styles and recordings. Richard Cook and Brian Morton's *The Penguin Guide to Jazz on CD, LP and Cassette* (London: Penguin, 1992) is a thoroughly comprehensive and sensitively written review of available recordings, indexed by artist. Other similar encyclopedic guides are available.

Although out of print, Brian Case and Stan Britt's *Illustrated Encyclopedia of Jazz* (New York: Crown, 1978) contains concise capsule biographies of a wide array of sax artists, many lesser-known. Ira Gitler's *Jazz Masters of the Forties* (New York: Da Capo, 1982) and Joe Goldberg's *Jazz Masters of the Fifties* (New York: Da Capo, 1983) both contain sections on the saxophone's progress in modern jazz. Now out of print, Leonard Feather's *The Book of Jazz from Then till Now* (New York: Bonanza Books, 1965) has three very informative chapters on the alto, tenor, and other saxophones.

OTHER RESOURCES

Saxophone Journal, a bimonthly magazine, is an invaluable resource for any saxophonist or aficionado, including interviews with prominent players, record reviews, buyers' guides, and a CD in every issue. It is published by Dorn Publications, Inc., Box 206, Medfield, MA 02052; (800) 527-6647. Dorn's Woodwind Service Catalog (available on request) has a wide selection of sax music, classical and jazz recordings, and instructional aids.

The North American Saxophone Alliance (NASA) is dedicated to academic music. Its activities include regional meetings featuring recitals and master classes, and the magazine *Saxophone Symposium*. Membership director for 1996 is Jonathan Helton, School of Music, Northwestern University, Evanston, IL 60208.

Instrument dealers specializing in saxophones advertise in *Saxophone Journal*. Mail-order catalog operations include The Saxophone Shop, 2834 Central St., Evanston, IL 60201, and The Woodwind & The Brasswind, 19880 State Line Rd., South Bend, IN 46637.

PHOTO CREDITS

Front cover: *Metronome* magazine. 3: Collection, Paul Cohen. 4–5: © Bob Willoughby 1995. 6: Herman Leonard. 7: Collection, Paul Cohen. 8: (left) Carl Lobel / Samuels Fine Art; (right) Institute of Jazz Studies, Rutgers University. 9: Culver Pictures. 10: Institute of Jazz Studies. 11: Collection, Richard Allen. 12: Bob Parent / Collection, Don Parent. 13: (top) Collection, Paul Cohen; (bottom) Collection, Dwight Deason. 14: Nancy Siesel / *New York Times Pictures*. 15: (center) Good Humor-Breyers Co.; (right) John Ficara / Sygma. 16: Culver Pictures. 17: Nick Knight. 18–19: (all) University of South Dakota, Shrine to Music Museum. 20: (all) Comité Internationale Adolphe Sax. 21: (left) University of South Dakota. 22: (top) University of South Dakota; (center, bottom) Collection, Paul Cohen. 23: (background) Collection, Paul Cohen; (foreground, all) Yamaha Corporation of America. 24–26: (all) Dave King / Collection, Paul Cohen. 27: (left, both) Dave King / Collection, Paul Cohen; (bottom center) Konstantin / Author's Collection; (bottom left) Collection, Paul Cohen. 28: Collection, Duncan P. Schiedt. 30: (center) Collection, Paul Cohen; (right) Smithsonian Institution, National Museum of American History. 31: (center) University of South Dakota; (right) *Musical America* magazine; (bottom) Collection, Barry Landau. 32: (top, center) University of South Dakota; (bottom) Institute of Jazz Studies. 33: (center) Collection, Duncan P. Schiedt; (bottom) University of South Dakota. 35: *Metronome* magazine. 36–39: Culver Pictures. 40: (top) Author's Collection; (bottom) Collection, Paul Cohen. 41: Charles Peterson / Collection, Don Peterson. 42: (top left) Collection, Frank Driggs; (bottom left) Charles Peterson / Collection, Don Peterson; (right) Institute of Jazz Studies. 43: (top) Charles Peterson / Collection, Don Peterson; (bottom) Collection, Frank Driggs. 44: (center) The Bettmann Archive; (right) University of South Dakota. 45: (both) University of South Dakota. 46: (top) Collection, Frank Driggs; (bottom) Smithsonian Institution. 47: Charles Peterson / Collection, Don Peterson. 48: Collection, Duncan P. Schiedt. 49–50: Charles Peterson / Collection, Don Peterson. 51: (top) Collection, Eugene Rousseau; (center) University of South Dakota; (bottom) Carl Fischer, Inc. 52: (background left) Rhythm magazine; (background right) Smithsonian Institution;

(left) Author's Collection; (top right) Author's Collection; (center right) Smithsonian Institution; (bottom right) *Metronome* magazine. 53: (background) Institute of Jazz Studies; (top) University of South Dakota; (right) Alastair Finlay/Author's Collection; (bottom) University of South Dakota. 54: (top) Collection, Frank Driggs; (bottom) *Metronome* magazine. 55: Charles Peterson / Collection, Don Peterson. 56: (center) Herman Leonard; (right) Institute of Jazz Studies. 57: (top) Collection, Frank Driggs; (bottom) Institute of Jazz Studies. 58: (top) Popsie Randolph / Collection, Frank Driggs; (bottom) Institute of Jazz Studies. 59: Popsie Randolph / Collection, Frank Driggs. 60: Author's Collection. 61: (top left) Author's Collection; (rest) Culver Pictures. 62–63: Bob Parent / Collection, Don Parent. 64: Larry Downing / Sygma. 65: Institute of Jazz Studies. 66: (both) Bob Parent / Collection, Don Parent. 67: (top, bottom) Institute of Jazz Studies; (right) Collection, Don Parent. 68–70: (all) Bob Parent / Collection, Don Parent. 71: John Abbott. 72–73: (button, statuette, tie, T-shirts) Alastair Finlay / Author's Collection; (CD101.9) WQCD-FM NYC; (chips) Zapps Potato Chip Company; (Five Spot, saxophonist/drummer) Bob Parent / Collection, Don Parent. 74 (top) RCA / Collection, Duncan P. Schiedt; (bottom) Val Wilmer. 75: Collection, Duncan P. Schiedt. 76: (left) Andrew Putler / Retna Ltd.; (center) Bob Parent / Collection, Don Parent; (right) Veryl Oakland / Retna Ltd. 77: John Abbott. 78: (left) Jeff Kravitz / Sygma; (center) Gene Martin / Retna Ltd.; (right) Bob Parent / Collection, Don Parent. 79: (left) Redferns; (right) Anthony Barboza. 80: (left) Dave Bilger; (center) San Francisco Saxophone Quartet; (right) Jay Blakesberg / Retna Ltd. 81: Salazar / Retna Ltd. 82–83: Les Jörgensen / Author's Collection. 84: Malcolm T. Liepke. 85: Les Jörgensen / Author's Collection. 86: Brooke-Alexander Galleries. 87: Larry Rivers. 88: Culver Pictures. 89: (top) King Features Syndicate; (right) Collection, Paul Cohen; (bottom left) 20th Century-Fox Film Corporation; (center left) Ben Sargent. 90: (left) Alastair Finlay / Mardi Gras Candies; (right) From the Hallmark Archives, Hallmark Cards Inc. 91: PTT Post BV. 92: Comité Internationale Adolphe Sax. 93: Jean-Christophe Poncelet. 94: Collection, Janet Nelson Harrington. 96: Todd Shapera. Jacket photo: Thomas Hooper.

I WANT TO THANK Paul Cohen, Frank Driggs, Dan Morgenstern and the Institute of Jazz Studies, Don Parent, Don Peterson, Duncan Schiedt, the Shrine to Music Museum, and Peter Tomlinson for their especially important help.

This book would have been impossible without the guidance and support of Mom and Dad and the belief of Ella and John, and a lot harder without the assistance of Julie, Jennifer, and the unflappable Leslie.

Paul Lindemeyer, pictured above with bassist Theo Wilson, is a freelance saxophonist and writer on jazz and popular music history. Originally from Ames, Iowa, he now lives in Ardsley-on-Hudson, New York.